W9-CCK-207

Bridges—Not Walls

BRIDGES
✒ NOT
WALLS

by Morris S. Lazaron

The Citadel Press
New York

To Hilda
our children
and grandchildren

CONTENTS

INTRODUCTION

O NE of the major tragedies in the world today is the fact that the great Religions, which ought to help unite mankind in mutual understanding and good will, divide mankind instead and add to our humanity's disunion their own special prejudices, animosities, and dogmatic fanaticisms. Within the last few generations science has created on this planet one neighborhood, where what happens anywhere matters everywhere, and where amity and goodwill are not moral luxuries but desperate necessities. If only the great Religions, instead of adding their own disagreements and dissensions to the world's confusion, could lead the way toward human brotherhood! If only they could focus attention on their major agreements, and could make the Golden Rule—which, in one form or another, they all teach—a working principle and not merely a pious sentiment!

It is this critical and sometimes frightening problem which Rabbi Lazaron faces in this book. Of course he finds no easy solution— there is none—but with courage and candor, with a sensitive conscience, an able mind, and warm goodwill, he has written a book which challenges the great Religions, especially Roman Catholicism, Protestantism, and Judaism in the United States, to amend their contentious ways.

This book is the more vital because it has boiled up out of the author's life-long experience. He is a rabbi, devoted to those basic faiths which make Judaism one of the world's great universal Religions, but throughout his long ministry he has practiced what this book preaches, finding friends across all religious lines, cooperating on common tasks with folk of other faiths, and striving

9

through organizations like the Conference of Christians and Jews to make religion a roadway to mutual understanding and respect. For many years he has been building bridges rather than walls, and now in this book he pleads the cause to which his life has been devoted.

One can easily imagine a man thus dedicated to the rapprochement of the world's various Religions, seeking that end by minimizing the differences which separate them. Some have tried that method. By diluting the distinctive factors of mankind's faiths, by proposing a thinned-out synthesis of ideas which all can accept, they have hoped to achieve harmony and even unity. Not so Rabbi Lazaron! He respects honest difference of opinion in religion as everywhere else. He is not asking anyone to surrender the cherished convictions of his faith. He proposes no synthetic blending of mankind's Religions on the basis of certain shared ideas. He expects Roman Catholics, Protestants, and Jews, Muslims, Buddhists, and Hindus, to continue holding distinctive ideas, and he makes plain his own loyal allegiance to Judaism. But still he pleads his cause: that the world's major faiths do share many deep convictions, that mutual understanding between them is of imperative importance, that they can work together for the common good, that instead of increasing the world's dissensions they can contribute to the world's peace and harmony, that the walls which divide them must be displaced by bridges of communication.

With such a cause to plead one can easily imagine an author avoiding controversial issues and speaking only in tones pleasant and agreeable. Not so Rabbi Lazaron! This is a plain-spoken and at times hard-hitting book. He candidly assails those elements in our Religions which make them embittered sources of discord rather than servants of peace and brotherhood. Writing as a Jew, he severely differs from Zionist nationalists who, so he judges, often identify Judaism with a political state and lose sight of its glory as a universal faith.

Only a few readers of this book, I suspect, will agree with everything in it, nor will the author expect them to. He constantly uses the personal pronouns—"I think," "It seems to me." This candid expression of personal conviction, often on debatable issues, is a major part of the book's charm and persuasiveness. The author does not make a roadway to mutual understanding and cooperation between our varied Religions by seeking detours around controversial matters. He dodges no difficulties, and his realistic facing of contentious issues is challenging. But still he pleads his cause: the tragic spectacle of mankind's major faiths adding to the world's bitterness and disorder cannot be endured; much of the dissension is caused by misunderstanding, prejudice, intolerance, bigotry; there are wide areas of agreement concerning spiritual values and ethical goals, and there are crucially important opportunities for cooperation and "togetherness" in serving mankind's good.

Writing as a Protestant Christian I hope that this book may have a wide reading. The author has been very merciful in dealing with us Christians, but he presents a challenge which should lead us to sterner judgments on ourselves. For the rising tide of the ecumenical movement and for all signs of increasing cooperativeness between the various Protestant denominations, and between Protestants and Roman Catholics, we have reason to be thankful. But there are too many of us Christians who are still manning the walls of religious bias and prejudice, as though Jesus had never spoken the Sermon on the Mount and Paul had never written the thirteenth chapter of First Corinthians. We Christians critically need bridges, not walls.

Harry Emerson Fosdick

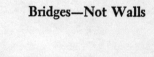

Bridges—Not Walls

CHAPTER ONE

Mostly Autobiographical

I AM Southern on both sides. My father was born in Atlanta, Georgia, and my mother in New Orleans. The Southern tradition is strong in me and my earliest memories are associated with hominy, hot bread, syrup and watermelon cuttings. My father's family had fled from Atlanta to Savannah with thousands of others when Sherman surrounded the city; and my uncle carried a bullet wound in his thigh from a northern shell which wrecked the Lazaron home on Peachtree Street. My mother's cousin was Judah P. Benjamin, Secretary of State of the Confederacy, whose "flight to destiny" has been so stirringly described by Dr. Alfred Hanna; and my maternal grandfather, Jacob Osorio De Castro, member of the Louisiana militia, New Orleans Home Guard, an unreconstructed rebel, refused to take the oath of allegiance to the United States which General Butler demanded when he stood at the gates of New Orleans; and had, therefore, to flee with his family to Mobile.

I have lived and worked and had some of the deepest joys of my life with the people of the South. One of my favorite memories centers around Tom Poole. Tom had been an old family servant. He was my friend and confidant and watched my growth with loving care. When I came home after my second year at the rabbinical seminary, Tom, like so many in their older age and baldness, had got "ligion." Tom was deacon of his church, and nothing would satisfy him but that his young charge should speak at his little church in Yammacraw, then on the outskirts of Savannah. How proud the old Negro was when on a hot August night, before a congregation that packed the edifice to the doors, he rose to introduce me, then all of eighteen. He told of his relation to the family and how he had raised me and in a final climax said, "I knows Mr. Morris from the day he was born. His face may be white, but his heart am black."

But the North was not a stranger to me, and some of my most exciting years were at the University of Cincinnati, when Dr. Charles William Dabney was president, and at the Hebrew Union College, the seminary for the training of reform rabbis. Many doors of the mind and heart were opened to me in these places. I found inspiration not only in the theological disciplines, but filled with an insatiable curiosity, I held imaginary conversations with Henry Van Dyke, Hamilton Wright Mabie, Kenneth Graham, John Fiske, E. H. Benson, John Dewey, William James and Josiah Royce whose books I read avidly. I played the violin and freshman football and sang in the Cincinnati May Festival the year they presented the Berlioz *Children's Crusade* and the Beethoven *Missa Solemnis*. I loved the theater and once a week I ushered at the Lyric, now a picture house, so that I could see the plays there. I took part in the production of *Antigone* and barnstormed through Ohio and Kentucky with the College Glee Club during spring recess.

My vacations were spent in Asheville, North Carolina. The local congregation was too small to afford a resident minister and therefore let me "supply" its pulpit when the town was filled with summer visitors. There for six years I practiced on an indulgent and long suffering congregation, learning something of the arts of preaching and teaching, all of which stood me in good stead when I was finally ordained in June, 1914, and accepted the invitation of the congregation at Wheeling, West Virginia, to become its minister.

During this testing period I took an occasional engagement to speak in other places in West Virginia, among them at Morgantown, seat of the State University. Arriving in the late afternoon, I strolled around the town and campus and noticed a number of placards with my picture, announcing the evening lecture. One of them particularly interested me. It was in the window of a drug store and was so strategically placed that the sign printed on the store window appeared across the mouth of this picture. The sign read, "Open Day and Night." The unconscious prophecy of that early experience has been more than fulfilled.

I stayed in Wheeling only nine months when in August, 1915, I was asked to occupy the pulpit of the Baltimore Hebrew Congregation, one of the oldest in the country. My comrades in the rabbinate, appalled at such rapid advance in one so raw and so young, described the change of pulpit as a record rabbinical high jump. After the first precarious landing, I stayed in Baltimore for thirty-four years, the full length of my active ministry.

In 1917, when our country was drawn into the first World War, and when Woodrow Wilson's ringing phrases brought hope to embattled peoples, I received a leave of absence to enlist as a chaplain in the army. Home on leave, my phone rang at two o'clock one morning. A voice said, "You a minister?" "Yes." "Well, I'm a soldier, Camp Meade. My outfit leaves noon today. My girl is here from Oklahoma; we want to get married. We looked in the phone book for the nearest minister and you are it. Coming right over." Bang, the receiver went down. By the time I had got dressed the front doorbell rang. I opened the door and there stood two doughboys and a girl. Obviously they were not Jewish. So I hesitated. One soldier said, "You the minister?" "Yes, but there seems to be some mistake. I'm a Jewish minister, a rabbi." Silence; then the prospective groom exploded, "Damn!" All ended happily however, as Fred Reynolds, a Methodist minister friend of mine and also an army chaplain, lived only three blocks away. He was routed out of bed and officiated at the obsequies of another bachelor.

Of all my friends among the ministers in Baltimore, none was closer than Hugh Birckhead, Rector of Immanuel Protestant Episcopal Church. He had come there from St. George's in New York and was as great in soul as he was in body. Until his untimely death, Hugh Birckhead was my most intimate friend among all the rabbis and clergymen of Baltimore. A fine figure of a man, over six feet tall, with strong chiselled features, he was a powerful preacher and a tender, solicitous pastor. He had done the up-to-then-unheard-of-thing—at least in Baltimore—of having me preach at one of his Sunday evening services, wearing my "Taleth" (prayer shawl) and gown. He told me there had been some discussion of the invitation among the officials of his congregation but that he had convinced them that no canonical law was involved, and he thought it would do both his and my congregations great good, aside from the personal happiness it would give him. The drama of the picture appealed to us both, that we should stand together, he in his vestments and I in mine. The service was conducted along traditional lines and I was to speak on Solomon's words at the dedication of the Temple. Immanuel Church was crowded that night with Christians and Jews. The choir sang Gounod's *Holy, Holy, Holy* and a Lewandowski number, *The Hallelujah*, from the liturgy of the synagogue. After it was over we went together into the robing room. Hugh stopped a moment to talk with one of his vestrymen, the late Brent Keyser. Mr. Keyser did not see me as I was standing behind him. I heard him say, "Well, it really was not too bad; in fact, ah—really it was—ah—quite good, a very successful and impressive service, Dr. Birckhead." A handsome admission from one who had opposed the project.

In 1921, with the unanimous consent of our wives, Hugh and I decided to make a pilgrimage to Palestine together. The announcement shook the city of Baltimore—started it talking. The late John Latane, then head of the history faculty at Johns Hopkins University could find no precedent for a Protestant minister and a rabbi making such a trip together. It was strange, unique, fantastic! The late Bishop Murray of the Protestant Episcopal Diocese of Maryland, was not so sure it was the "correct and proper" thing to do. Betting, they say, began in the clubs of the town as to *who* was coming back *what*. Was Lazaron coming back a Christian or was Birckhead coming back a Jew? Finally it was decided to call off all bets because, it was said, if anyone converted, surely it would be Lazaron, because in his case the transition could be effected with less physical discomfort!

* * *

It was night in Jerusalem. Hugh and I stood silent on Mount Olives. We had talked with Zionist and Arab, Jewish, Moslem and Christian leaders and government officials. Even then, thirty-eight years ago, suspicion, tension and anger rose like forbidding walls and our hearts were heavy with foreboding.

We looked out on the Holy City. The moon was full and spun a web of silver loveliness over the earth. The white buildings which, while reflecting the pitiless sun of an August day wearied the eyes with their hot, insistent brilliance, now glowed in the magic mesh of moonlight. The sharp outlines of towers and wall softened. Domes and minarets of mosque and church and synagogue lifted themselves above the lines of houses and seemed to melt away as they rose through the translucent curtain of the descending sky. Out of the stillness and beauty, a great peace came to us.

Ghost figures walked the pathways of the heavens, prophet and psalmist chanting in ghost language all their dreams and hopes, which man had neglected or ignored. Moses, Amos, Hosea, Jeremiah, Isaiah, Micah, Jesus, Mohammed. They walked together the radiant pathways of the stars and chanted the litany: "One God in all the universe, one humanity on earth!"

The stunted trees around us seemed to take more substantial form. They stirred to movement as a cool breeze came up from below. Two figures appeared: one seated, head on knees, who seemed to be asleep; the other standing. And the one who was standing touched the shoulder of him who was seated, spoke to him and we could hear the words he spoke:

"What, thou sleepest?

Couldst thou not wait with me one hour?"

Hugh Birckhead and I clasped hands that night on the Mount of Olives, overlooking Jerusalem. He had heard and seen what I had heard and seen and each of us knew. We clasped hands. And we knew that one man's watching is not enough. And we knew that two men's watching is not enough. Not one hour, but years, a lifetime. And not two men, but many men. Hugh Birckhead is dead. And I watch. But I do not watch alone. For many have seen the visions and heard the voices.

* * *

How deeply gratifying has been my life as a minister, for life has been good to me. I have known plaudit, honor, and praise, which of course have helped; but I have also known condemnation and prejudice and abuse, which have hurt. But when the sum is totaled and the balance made, I know that life has been good to me, better than to most, and has been best of all in those times when my soul went out to meet another in one burning moment of poignant recognition.

I spoke the truth as I saw it. Sometimes it met with favor, especially in the earlier years. Then in the later years the truth as I saw it was a protest against the trends and tendencies of the times. To turn against the tide is not easy. It often means the sacrifice of influence, recognition, some of the honors of the world, the consideration of many colleagues, and the regard of erstwhile friends and contemporaries. I have made the sacrifice with my eyes open, but I am happy in the choice. I would choose to do the same again.

No matter how plentiful were disappointments and heartaches, I had no illusions concerning myself and my own shortcomings and I did not find it too hard to make allowances for others. To stand the last watch with a man while his mate drifted out; with a parent when his child was dying; to consecrate two young people in marriage, to confirm or marry their children; to have the privilege of trying to bring some measure of healing and strength in sorrow, some bit of courage to face grim duties, some inspiration for useful kindly living; to have the privilege of trying to evoke sensitivity to truth and beauty and holiness, and occasionally to see the light come into eyes beholding for the first time a vision of what life could be; to reach at things beyond the grasp of man, but to know that the merit is in the reach, not the attainment; to try to make youth feel that all they dream and know of decency, honor and justice is real and the striving to achieve them the supreme duty of man; to hold to this truth despite the coldness, pettiness, smugness, meanness, cruelty and brutality of men; to proclaim the living word of righteousness and brotherhood amid the clamor, the misery and the wickedness in the world; to try to give strength to the weak, hope to the hesitant, faith to the doubting—these are the real compensations in the minister's life.

The true minister is always a child at heart, no matter how sophisticated he may be; and when his spirit loses the quality of wonder at the mystery of life, the sense of goodness in every man and woman, the feeling that he is a very part of an eternal unfolding fellowship which in the end will bind the hearts of the people by the golden threads of love, if he loses this radiant vision, his work is done.

In the fall of 1933, a strange and unprecedented sight appeared in many of the cities of the nation. A Protestant minister, a Catholic priest and a rabbi stood together on the same platform in schools and colleges and public meetings and churches and synagogues and discussed the differences between the Religions, the irritations, suspicions and prejudices among the major faiths. Dr. Everett R. Clinchy, the late Father John Eliot Ross and I toured the country under the auspices of the National Conference of Christians and Jews. *Time* magazine called the trio, "The Flying Ministerial Circus." This was the first of many such trios and perhaps set the pattern so commonly accepted and seen today. The idea was to promote understanding and amity between the faiths and among the followers of the Judeo-Christian tradition by a public demonstration. It was something new in the history of the Religions.

At one such meeting at a city in the Far West, 2800 high school pupils were assembled. After the priest, the minister and I had finished speaking, the young people were invited to ask questions. The response was immediate. "Father Ross, what about the Catholic opposition to intermarriage?" Father Ross explained the Catholic position. One youngster remarked that, as one committed to celibacy, it was hardly proper for the priest to voice judgment about the love of a youth for a maid. Quick as a flash Father Ross replied, "Well it doesn't take a chicken to judge an egg."

On another occasion a question was shot at me. "Why do all Jews think and act alike and together?" To which I replied, "The only thing two Jews can agree upon is what a third Jew should give to charity."

These, of course, were surface and superficial incidents which in no way detracted from the major emphasis of the undertaking, which was to tear down walls of ignorance and to build bridges of appreciation, at the same time preserving the integrity of each denominational group.

I often declared that it was to the everlasting glory of the vast Protestant majority that recognizing its responsibility and obligation as the dominant group, it initiated and supported the interfaith movement, so democratic and American in aim and spirit.

The trio faced an exhausting four-day program in Chicago, often appearing before six and eight audiences beginning at nine o'clock in the morning at some school assembly and ending with an evening public meeting. The Chicago World's Fair was on at the same time, the fall of 1933, and Clinchy, Ross and I determined to take a night off. At dinner in one of the restaurants at the Fair grounds we were recognized, for a friendly press had generously publicized our visit. Greatly embarrassed, we tried to beat a hasty retreat when the proprietor of the dining place came over to us and begged us to remain. "We are having the orchestra play something in your honor," he told us. Reluctantly we consented to remain and listen. A few minutes later, after a ringing announcement and a flourishing fanfare, the orchestra played, of all things, "The Last Roundup," while the crowd joined in singing, "Git along little dogie, git along, git along."

This is the halcyon day of the demagogue. Times of great change breed men and women who use the ignorance, the fears, the suspicions and the prejudices which divide us to promote their own selfish aims. Our democracy, one of the greatest experiments in human relations in history, can be destroyed in a generation if we do not learn to live together in justice and cooperation and peace. We have to know enough, to feel deeply enough, and to be wise enough to sift the chaff from the wheat, to differentiate the spurious defender of democracy who speaks with the tongue of angels, from the real defender of the liberties of men, to reject the former and follow the latter in humility and courage. This is the testing time of faith in the open mind, in the invincible quest for truth and the will to human fellowship, a faith which must be applied in all our relationships—economic, political, racial and religious—else we might go the way of Rome and Carthage.

A ministry of nearly thirty-five years in one city and in one congregation offered ample opportunity not only to test the validity of my hopes and convictions but to apply them. My ministry in Baltimore naturally brought me into intimate contact with people as human beings. I found much that was dark and sinister, but much also that was illumined and open. I found much that was selfish, and mean and ignoble; but also much that was generous, exalting and brotherly.

We accept prejudice and ill-feeling among men as a fact in life, and it is a fact. But why should we not accept also as a fact that prejudice and ill-feeling may be mitigated if we make more than a half-hearted effort to overcome them? I have found such effort an exciting experience.

In Baltimore I worked with other religious groups, exchanged pulpits with rabbis and Protestant ministers and enjoyed the friendship of my brother ministers, Protestant and Catholic.

In my entire ministry there have been two transcendent themes. I have earnestly sought to find some common ground for unity among Jews amid all the varying cultural, national, linguistic strains, the differing interpretations of Judaism, the often violently opposite reactions to current events which divide them; and I have wanted, as far as possible, to help effect some measure of reconciliation between Christian and Jew. In the first of these aims I fear that I have not succeeded. As events unfolded, I was forced to abandon the search for a common ground among my fellow Jews chiefly on the question of Jewish political nationalism and to take a position of unqualified opposition to its intrusions on the American scene.

In the second of these aims I have earned, I feel, a measure of success; in my work as a rabbi in Baltimore, as a chaplain in the Army, as a member of trios touring the country under the auspices of the National Conference of Christians and Jews, and in all my relations with people of various faiths.

Furthermore, whatever I have accomplished in this regard has been due, I believe, to my faith as a Jew. The reality of God, the universality of religion—spelled with a small r—the relation between religion and the Religions, between faith and reason, the importance of reason as the great corrector and the function of religion in the life of the individual and the nation—all these themes, deriving from my conception of religion and Judaism, are the content of this book. The shortcomings and failures of the Religions and their followers as well as their achievements will be discussed. And I have drawn upon the experience of a long ministry to point out how religion can be a more effective and inspiring influence in the personal life and in the nation.

What I shall say is the expression of my own personal and deep conviction. I can only hope that it represents the conviction of a courageous group of men and women in this country who will be willing to face the animosity, the prejudice, and the opposition of large groups lacking understanding of our common ground and our common needs. The recommendations I offer cannot be considered as the official position of any single group. Growing out of my experience as man and minister, I heartily propose them to those who are interested in solving the pressing problem of how men and women of various cultural, national, racial and religious backgrounds can live together cooperatively in this decisive hour in the history of our American democracy.

I want to talk to you about our country and about its people. I have noticed a tenseness in the bearing of men and a weariness in their eyes. Voices are shrill, nerves are taut, tempers are quick; we are losing patience with each other. The ground is being prepared and seeds are being sown and a harvest of misery may be reaped unless we plough up the weeds and plant seeds of confidence, hope and faith in ourselves, in each other and in the future.

The wholesomeness of our national spirit is set upon not only by enemies outside. Our worst enemies are perhaps those of our own household because they attack the bases of our faith in democracy. Their motivation is either a fanatic dogmatism that brooks no difference or an unreasoning romanticism which expects Utopia, come sun-up. We are told that modern culture has collapsed, that liberalism is passé. The constant barrage batters down our resistance, undermines our stamina, weakens our faith in our own institutions and causes us to look for someone or something to blame for our own shortcomings and failures.

Do not let us give hospitality in our minds and hearts to the enemies within, purveyors of hate, messengers of despair. The way is not back, it is forward. What we need in our country is less agitation and more restraint, less unbridled emotionalism and more sobriety, less indulgence in feelings and more self-discipline, less fear and more confidence, less looking elsewhere for Utopia and more faith in ourselves and our institutions. To this restraint, sobriety and self-discipline, to this faith in the free, liberated intelligence and its power to maintain a democracy it has created, I summon you, for the welfare of the nation and to the glory of God.

CHAPTER TWO

Conversation in London

HE spoke quietly and his eyes looked beyond us as if we were not there.

"Now for the first time in my life I begin to know what Moses and Jesus were talking about."

This London publisher, head of a firm some generations old, was having tea with us at Dartmouth House in London. It was fall, 1941. The blitzes of the preceding May had leveled acres of ground around St. Paul's, and his establishment near the Cathedral was wiped out. He was, economically speaking, ruined; for it was not possible, in war-time England, to replace the elaborate presses and machinery of his large plant. We were silent as he paused and then continued speaking.

"To me as to most men Moses and Jesus were familiar, even cherished names; but they were not real and the people to whom they spoke were not real. My world was a fighting world where men asked and gave no quarter. Neither the thunders of Sinai nor the gentle voice from the mount could be heard in the ruthless battles. Religious sentiments were praiseworthy; they should be spoken in churches and synagogues and should be taught to children. But they had no meaning in the market place, nor could they be practical rules of conduct for men or nations. They were sweet illusions to which the weak and the wounded, the bruised, the beaten lifted their eyes for healing. The brave and the strong did not need them. That night of the blitz my wife and I stood some blocks away and saw everything we had built over many years go down in the bombing and the burning.

"It is not easy to see such a thing as this. It was as if the very ground under our feet had melted away and we were left standing on nothingness. We looked at each other and said not a word, but we knew what was in each other's heart. No longer the easy comfortable lives, the pleasant regimen of an ordered existence in a reasonably safe world. Nothing was left to us of our old life. Everything would be different.

"We would have to begin again, and we did not think that we could do it; but there were some things the bombs did not destroy and the fires did not burn, some things that were left, things that did not have anything to do with our previous living or our present comfort. We had taken them so much for granted. They were left; they did not burn—our love for our children, our devotion to each other, the same friends, the modest joys of reading, conversation, evenings in our home—none of these things had been consumed in the catastrophe. They were left to us; and we did not know how much they could possibly mean. They remained, and in time were transformed with a strange loveliness.

"Actually we had much less, but we seemed to have more. What we thought was love had drawn a line and closed us in with what we loved. It was a sort of fence that shut out the world. It was a wall between us and those others that were different. We came to learn that love is not a fence, not a wall, but rather a bridge. We began to tear down the fences and the walls; we began to build bridges. We looked at men and women with different eyes. We seemed to feel something of their struggle and their pain, to sense something of their sacrifices. Pity filled our hearts when they failed. Joy gladdened us when they succeeded. We began to look at people as human beings. We did not seem to see their color, their creed, the clothes they wore; we did not hear the language they spoke. We looked at them as human persons, ones who, like us, were caught up in circumstances which, alone, they had no power to change. They were weak, alone, and so were we weak and alone. But in us both there was some strength and the little strength that was theirs and the little that was ours, when brought together with that of many others, could be a great strength, an invincible power that might batter down all the fences and all the walls, and build the bridges that could unite the world. Now we are happier than we have ever been before. Yes, for the first time in my life, I begin to understand what Moses and Jesus were talking about."

CHAPTER THREE

Religion and the Religions

In dream I saw two Jews that met by chance,
One old, stern-eyed, deep-browed, yet garlanded
With living light of love around his head.
The other young, with sweet seraphic glance,
Around went on the town's satanic dance,
Hunger a-piping while at heart he bled.
Shalom Aleichem mournfully each said,
Nor eyed the other straight and looked askance.

Sudden from church outrolled an organ hymn,
From synagogue a loudly chanted air,
Each with its prophet's high acclaim instinct.
Then for the first time met their eyes, swift-linked,
In one strange, silent, piteous gaze, and dim,
With bitter tears of agonized despair.

Moses and Jesus *by* ISRAEL ZANGWILL

PERHAPS we, too, all of us, you and I and all the nations and peoples of the world, will have to begin to understand what Moses and Jesus were talking about. For, instead of uniting men and teaching them the real meaning of brotherhood, our Religions have often become divisive forces; and credal and denominational ambitions have mocked that brotherhood which is prayed for and preached from every pulpit. "Believe this, do that, the sabbath is

Friday, Saturday or Sunday, drink the wine, eat the wafer, lay phylacteries and keep kosher; be circumcised, dipped, totally immersed, or sprinkled; say Mass or Kaddish or grind out your prayers on the wheel!" How often has our Religion become only a personal, fleeting emotional experience, rather highly paid for, that one may receive on Friday, Saturday or Sunday; one far removed from the practical dilemmas of life and the heartaches and struggles of the masses of men and women.

If these things are sometimes true, it is you and I who are guilty, not the other fellow and guilty also is every occupant of pulpit and pew anywhere, whose intellectual indolence protests against too great mental activity and whose constrained point of view blinds him to the social tasks of religion. We are all of us responsible for the tragic plight of thousands of consecrated priests, ministers and rabbis whose livelihood is dependent upon their hewing to the line of our theological authoritarianisms and our economic prejudices. We have sometimes made moral cowards of our finest spirits and driven prophecy from church and synagogue at a moment in history when we need it most. We are all of us guilty. And that is why I urge that you and I and all the nations and peoples of the world begin to understand what Moses and Jesus were talking about.

To do this we must enter into a close and critical appraisal of the meaning of religion in our daily lives. In these days every custom, every tradition, every cherished institution, and every generally accepted idea is summoned before the court of reason, utility or truth. It must prove itself reasonable, it must prove itself useful and, in so far as it can, it must prove itself true. The Religions are not and should not be excepted from this present critical appraisal. There are, however, some who will object to submitting their Religions to such tests. To do so, they say, would introduce anarchy or would destroy the authority of the Religions and the moral laws they enjoin. For my part, I respect the sincerity of such criticism, but I believe the fears to be unfounded. For the creative spirit of man which will not be chained, is breaking through our current opinions, our uncritically accepted dogmatic assumptions, and revitalizing all our values, seeking thereby to express itself in newer forms. A great deal of good will issue from the reconsideration and reexamination of the meaning of religion and the Religions in our daily life.

One striking instance of such good occurring from critical examination of religious commitments occurs to me. I once invited the late Daniel E. Willard and a number of other distinguished Baltimoreans to address the men of my congregation. I had in mind the salutary influence exerted by the example of men of affairs in whose daily life religion had deep significance. It is not an easy thing to put into words the intangible spiritual purposes which guide one's life. But Mr. Williard's address, though it was unorthodox, showed the struggle of an innately religious man as he fought his way from man-made dogma representing itself as divinely revealed truth, through unbelief, back to the foundations upon which all the Religions are based. His address was a thrilling record of his spiritual anabasis. The *Baltimore Sun* reported the address at generous length. Then many letters appeared in the Forum column castigating Mr. Willard unmercifully because he rejected the dogmatic assertions of evangelical Christianity even though he had summarized his convictions by saying, "I believe in the Fatherhood of God, the brotherhood of man and the leadership of Jesus."

Of course, if one believes that God has revealed the means of salvation—whatever that may mean—to one denomination and to it alone; if one believes that those who are outside one credal group are damned—whatever that may mean—one could be deeply irritated by Mr. Willard's remarks. But if a person believes that in the universe there are mind and will and law and purpose and love, the synthesis of which we call God, if one believes that every sect represents an effort to understand God, but that none can completely comprehend him; if one believes that in a very real sense all men are brothers because they are children of that God, and if because of these beliefs one resolves to live in sympathy and helpfulness with one's fellows, if one believes these things, then

Mr. Willard's address takes on profound meaning and significance. Though critical and unorthodox and unacceptable to many, a great deal of good and of inspiration came from his stirring story as he addressed my congregation in Baltimore.

Is it not possible in this world for those who walk humbly with God, the completeness of whose reality none of us can utterly understand—is it not possible for those who say they believe in God to live so that their belief becomes fact and truth in their own lives, can be expressed to others, and shared with them, as Mr. Willard's was? What a miracle would take place in this world if men concerned themselves not so much with pontificating over what others should believe, but rather with expressing in their own lives the noblest imperatives of their own personal beliefs. This alone is true humility, and when it departs from our sanctuaries, arrogance comes in to take its place. Doubt is the great corrective even though but a temporary one, an overnight stopping place in the pilgrimage of the soul, one that must lead to deeper things, one that ought to make us continually aware of our need for humility and of our need for a critical examination of our beliefs. In this respect agnosticism must be a constant therapeutic element in all real religion. Not agnosticism as to God's existence, but one as to whether any other person or group can ever comprehend or explain the mysteries of God and man and life in their entirety. ". . . a man's reach should exceed his grasp, or what's a Heaven for?"

The reader may feel that my prejudice against theology is somewhat exaggerated. To explain my position I recall what Voltaire said to Frederick the Great, "Perhaps humanity which is the principle of all my thoughts has beguiled me." Perhaps, I might say, God and humanity, which are the principles of all my thoughts, have beguiled me.

I stand amazed and reverent before the intellectual energy with which great minds have labored in the field of theology, seeking ultimate answers to the persisting questions. What is this world and the universe of which it is a part? What is man? What is the meaning of life? The theologians are among the great explorers. They follow unmarked trails in the undiscovered country whose boundaries are the farthest reaches of the human spirit. God's whisper came to them as it came to Kipling's explorer, "Something's lost beyond the ranges, lost and waiting for you, go." They brought back a report to us less daring and more earthbound. The guidance of their grand designs has brought healing, hope and faith to men, which they expressed not only in religious insights, systematically presented in our theologies, but in shrines, in Balbek, the Agora, in the Taj Mahal and the music of the Missa Solemnis, and the glory of the Sistine Madonna, and in the incomparable grandeur of the Jewish Day of Atonement.

I stand amazed and reverent before all this and yet my prejudice against theology derives from the all too frequent absolute nature of its presumptions. To me, every systematic theology is but the effort of one man, or a group of men, to set forth what it believes about God, man and the world. Every theological system has won devotion from some men, but theologies have also resulted in religious controversy and even irreligious conduct, possibly because of the absolute nature of their presuppositions, when the followers of one or another system felt that forcible conversion or extermination of opponents was necessary to their salvation or the world's good.

Perhaps it is not pious to do so but I have often wondered what God would say to those who speak with utter finality in his name.

The contemplation of the millions in India, China, Japan and the islands of the Far East, who developed cultures, civilizations and religions, and who produced great literature and art, yet who are without the law of Jew and Gentile, but within the law of Mohammed, Buddah and Confucius, should make us followers of Moses and Jesus somewhat less dogmatic in our assumptions. I say I have often wondered what God would say to them who speak with such finality of authority in his name. Would he inquire with the becoming restraint one usually attributes to deity, "How do you know so completely what is in my mind?" The question is not unreasonable in a more or less rational universe because even the most orthodox theologians attribute rationality to grand design.

I share the feeling of a physician friend of mine who said, "The trouble with people is not that they do not know things, but that they know so many things wrong."

We may be loathe to admit it, but we have believed that steel girders, sanitary plumbing, television, the atom bomb, all our vast physical and intellectual resources, our technical know-how which seems to contribute stability to our illusory religious view of things, will somehow save us. These are our gods and we have bowed down to them in adoration, an adoration which is no less appalling than that of the Hottentot who carves an image in wood, the work of his own hand, and declares, "This is my god."

What we need is a certain apartness, an objectivity, a disinterestedness, and above all a deep and abiding conviction that there is in this world a supreme spirit whose instruments we are, manifesting itself in the dreams and hopes of men for truth, beauty and holiness; that to ignore or to violate or reject that spirit in its manifestations in human life is to root out of the lives of men and women an incentive potent enough to make those dreams and hopes come true.

The vast machinery of collective human life derives its driving force from the same law of harmony which the pealing organ obeys. Society moves forward in those moments in history when men strive to apply in their relations with each other the sympathy, understanding and brotherhood that all human experience proclaims to be the goals of life. Our rude squabbling, name-calling, and turbulent warring among each other have caused us to forget this most important fact.

It is not only difference of opinion (political, economic or religious) that creates the social injustice, the class hatred and the wars that blight our era; it is rather the closed mind, first breeding suspicion of the different, then dislike of it, which finally builds the walls that bar the way to fellowship. Our need is not to sink differences; our need is to distinguish between the presumptions of our particular Religion and the pride, prejudices and uninformed animosities which grow out of those presumptions. The Religions and their followers must learn that their strength is not in the increase of their authority but in the deepened humility and the moral greatness of their devotees. When these shall have been achieved, perhaps we will understand what Moses and Jesus were talking about.

It is said today that we need more religion, that our crisis is a spiritual one, that man's scientific knowledge has outstripped his moral strength. We have heard and read these words so often that their sound has become dully familiar. Many of us repeat them, perfunctorily, insensitive to their meaning; and many Catholics begin to count their beads, Protestants to sing their doxology, Jews to recite the Great Confession on the day of Atonement, in the same spirit that an Indian peasant turns his prayer wheel. Having done such things, these people count themselves religious. But true religion is more than this. True religion is the most revolutionary influence in the world. More powerful than guns or bombs, it can make the world a paradise in our generation. It is this kind of religion that Moses and Jesus were talking about; for though Moses and Jesus spoke their own language and at one time and one place to one people, no one period heard them, no one land gave them birth. They were revolutionaries meant for all time. Yet though we say we reverence them and say we accept their leadership today, many Christians and Jews have little understanding of what they said and less readiness to accept what they said even when they do understand it. Should Jesus come to our country today, he would knock on many doors which would be shut in his face, he would find many places where he would not be permitted to lay his head; and should Moses come to our country today, he would be labelled by Jews a trouble-maker and a controversial figure to be avoided and shunned.

The present world tension is not only a struggle between contending imperialisms, between Washington and Moscow, between East and West, between Communism and Capitalism; it is larger than an effort to save Roman Catholics and Catholicism in Russia and the Russian-occupied nations, to save Protestants and Protestantism in Soviet-dominated areas and in Italy, Spain and Latin America, to save Jews and Judaism in Israel and lands less blest than ours. It is a wider and deeper struggle involving all races and nations, creeds, cultures and colors of men. It manifests itself in all areas of man's economic, political, social and religious life, and in the hearts of men. Of that struggle shall we be witnesses only? Past and present warn us. Peter sat by the fire and warmed himself, and Nero played while Rome burned, and Russian orthodox priests discussed minutiae of dogma while the Bolsheviks let loose a bloodbath. And the Bishop of Rome blessed Italian troops in the rape of Abyssinia and made a treaty with Hitler. And Protestant ministers condemned their brother ministers as backsliders and renegades, teachers of false doctrines and Communists. Jews slandered Jews, rabbis denounced their brother rabbis and closed their pulpits and their hearts to them; and Jews suffered their Arab brothers to languish in camps, while Jews, Moslems and Christians killed each other.

Religion and religionists have a place in all these struggles. Indeed, religion in its largest dimensions has a supreme place in this epic conflict. But it is not enough for the Religions to be on the right side, they must be on the right side in the right spirit; not only with sound but with sense, not only with passion but with pity, not only with conviction but with conscience, not with hate but with humility. Only when religion does have such a place and the Religions such a spirit, will we begin to understand what Moses and Jesus were talking about.

I do not wish to destroy the faith of anyone. I would not take from any man the strength that comes to him from what he believes or the convictions for which I respect and honor him. He is a better man because he roots his conduct in the disciplines of his faith. It is not rejection I seek, but a sense of proportion. I would give religion and the various Religions their due and proper place in the vast perspectives which are open to the seekers of truth. I have neither knowledge enough nor insight enough to dare to say mine is true and yours is false, mine is right and yours is wrong.

For religion is a matter of universal experience and any particular Religion, such as Christianity or Judaism or Mohammedanism is but an interpretation of this universal experience. This fact need not minimize the importance of those convictions which attach to particular interpretations of religion, even when they present themselves as the truth, the whole truth and nothing but the truth; for I do not reject or summarily dismiss interpretations of religion. There are value and truth in all of them.

But if someone should say, "My religion can be proved," it might easily be asked, "Can it?" Would the proof offered be acceptable to the unbiased mind? And if one should say, "My religion is a matter of personal experience, and therefore it is truth"; it can easily be replied, "It is truth for you who experience it but only for you."

Or if someone should say, "My religion is a matter of revelation," one need only ask, "How is revelation to be defined? Will revelation be limited to what is said to one person or one group, in one place or at one time?" Revelation is a process, a continuing unfolding; it is man's expanding apprehension of reality, one which knows no race or creed or color, one which came to the American Indian and the African Negro and the yellow man of Asia as it came to Moses and to Jesus and to Mohammed. It is found in art, in music and in literature. Is it to be imprisoned in a creed, chained to a sacrament or a ceremony? Expressed in a setting, however beautiful in church or synagogue, in mosque or cathedral, shall it be said of it, this and this alone is true? To such assertions revelation itself will reply, "No, I am but the messenger of the Lord of the universe. I speak a universal language."

Thus, what is said about revelation is a matter of personal faith. It is acceptance. My acceptance or your acceptance of our own or someone's belief as truth which comes from God.

It is precisely in this area where difficulties between the various faiths begin. Each Religion assumes that it is the recipient of some special revelation. It does not necessarily deny that God revealed himself to other Religions but it declares that these other revelations are in some way only partial or incomplete; that to *it* has been revealed the full and final insight into God's will for man. Judaism, particularly in its orthodox and conservative, less than in its liberal or reform expression, conceives itself as such a revealed religion. Christianity, both Catholic and Protestant, conceive themselves likewise as revealed Religions.

Orthodox and conservative Judaism declare God revealed himself to Moses and "there has been no prophet like unto Moses." God further revealed himself in the Pentateuch and in the Bible, every word of which has some deep meaning; the interpretations of the rabbis in successive generations are true and point the way of life for men. Israel stands in special relation to God, his messenger, his witness, his servant. Traditional Judaism as a revealed Religion has evolved a sort of Jewish trinity, God, Jew and the State of Israel, and the greatest of these is Israel! The rules and regulations, the forms and ceremonies, which the Jew must observe, are for the purification of the Jew so he will be fit to continue to be God's witness till that day when all the nations will accept the ethical monotheism of Judaism. "The Lord shall be one and His name shall be one." This is the way and the life revealed by God through Judaism for the redemption of man.

The Roman Catholic concept of revelation is quite similar. An explanation of it was given in a sermon preached in St. Patrick's Cathedral by a certain Father Donohee on October 15, 1955. Father Donohee, a member of the Cathedral clergy staff, said, "The one church that Christ established is where Peter is today," and he called upon Roman Catholics to resist the persistent clamor of the creedless that one Religion is as good as another. According to Father Donohee, saying that one Religion is as good as another, is tantamount to saying that no god is as good as the living God. He further asserted, "No amount of broad-mindedness can alter the fact that any church that contradicts the Catholic church cannot be the true church." He went on to say that "Pope Pius XII was the only man in the whole wide world who can even claim to be St. Peter's successor; for in his hands, we find the keys of the kingdom. There, too, we find the mandate from Christ to teach all nations. The Bishop of Rome with the other bishops of the Catholic Church is alone the custodian of the entire doctrine of Christ. They alone are the true successors of the apostles. If then there is only one church established by Christ with Peter as the pastor, the whole world for its parish, Christ's complete doctrine as its sermon until the end of time, what is there left for any other church?"

Likewise with Protestantism. Protestantism as a revealed Religion makes a similar claim to exclusive knowledge of God's will as revealed in the Old and New Testaments. I remember a conversation I had with saintly men who were utterly convinced that the Bible is the final revealed word of God. They had dedicated their lives to promoting the fulfillment of what they believed to be the revelation of God's will. They accepted every word of the Bible as literally true. The prophets they said, were told of the coming of the Messiah, Jesus; and this they preached. There will be a second coming which, they asserted, will be marked by a return of the Jew to Palestine and the acceptance by the Jew of Jesus as Savior. The pattern of contemporary events, the establishment of the State of Israel, seem to them to fulfill the assumptions of this theology. Perhaps the details attendant upon and following the creation of the state, were awkwardly out of harmony with the divine plan, but the first step had been taken toward the day of Jesus' second coming to judge the nations and build the kingdom of God. For this reason all of them abhorred anti-Semitism. "We no longer want conversion of the Jews," they said, "but conversation with them, that together, in the spirit of Jesus we may fulfill the prophecies." The sincerity of my friends made discussion difficult. I could only point out as gently as possible that we started from different premises, that for this reason there was no basis for argument. I could not accept what they believed to be revealed truth; it was a matter of personal faith for them.

The same dissent must be entered in reference to most liberal

Protestant thinkers. For all their rational and critical approaches to Protestant theology, they revert to the phrases and vocabulary of evangelical Christianity and its theological schematisms. They attempt to express the substance of archaic dogma in modern language. They speak of sin, suffering, atonement and redemption, but in the framework of a Christology which they naturally accept as revelation because they are Christians.

For instance, Dr. Paul Tillich, one of the outstanding Protestant theologians, in his *Existence in the Christ,* starts with the estrangement of man from God; Jesus the Christ brings reconciliation. These are the central motivations of his theology. But for me the Bible legend of the fall of man reveals the moment centuries ago in the pilgrimage of the Jewish soul when it felt estrangement from the divine being and the necessity for reconciliation. As the record of a spiritual experience expressed in terms our ancestors could understand, it is meaningful. It has a poignant beauty as of someone partly blinded but groping through the dark toward a light. For us today the story of the Garden of Eden symbolizes the difference between what a man is and what he wants to be, or what he hopes to be, or what he dreams of being.

The critical mind cannot resist pointing out that the ideas of sin, suffering, atonement and redemption, are universal. They are found in other religious insights. Judaism, for instance, has conceptions of sin, suffering, atonement and redemption. Why should these Christian interpretations of these concepts be proclaimed as final and unmistakably divine and exclusive revelations of the meaning of life? They are, indeed, for those who believe them so to be, but for them only.

Revelation in these various phases is a matter of personal experience which reaches beyond what we can see or hear. It is what we most deeply believe, and about which there can be no argument. For men walk different trails; some see a summit of religious experience from the West and others from the East; but each of them describes what his eyes behold, seeing the same peak, but from different viewpoints.

Shall we not therefore agree that while our faiths may differ, they all spring out of the wonder we all feel as we contemplate the mystery of life, out of the sense of relation we feel to the source of all existence? Though our faiths may differ, they are the answers that we, as persons, have found most satisfying to the persistent questions: What is Man? What is the meaning of Life? What is the goal of human endeavor? And in the final analysis, are they not human answers, with all the limitations our mortal being puts on them? These basic propositions have a great deal to do with the future of our country and the world. Once granted, the task of reconciliation between members of various Religions, races and colors can be begun everywhere.

A concrete instance of the need for such reconciliation occurs to me in reflecting on my experience as a chaplain in World War I. I had been sent to the Chaplains' Training School at Camp Taylor near Louisville, Kentucky. Several hundred ministers of all denominations from all parts of the nation were there. After a few days, some of us, finding ourselves congenial spirits, sat together in the evenings telling stories of personal experience that ministers tell, and discussing things holy and profane in which we were interested. It was such a varied assortment as only the service can bring together—a Presbyterian, an Episcopalian, a Catholic priest, a Methodist, a Baptist, a Unitarian, a Christian Scientist, and two rabbis. All of us were men of some sophistication. But most of the ministers in our barracks came from smaller towns and country districts; they were sincere men but somewhat less than liberal in their attitudes toward religion. They came to our corner and listened to the conversation. Some, shaking their heads in dismay, hurriedly left us; but others lingered, open-mouthed.

One evening the talk was about dogma and creed. In the frank interchange of ideas, when many unorthodox views had been voiced, I expressed my own convictions. At that moment an evangelist named Law, a huge fellow, lean of limb with high forehead and eyes shining with the light of conviction, rose from where he had been sitting and said something that got my rabbinical goat.

"Law," I replied, "you do not mean to suggest seriously that if I do not believe as you believe, accept the Religion that you accept, that I will be damned?" Law drew himself up to his great height, took his testament from his tunic pocket, read a few verses, and in a most solemn voice declared, "Yes, Rabbi, if you do not believe these things, you will be damned." An awkward silence of astonishment followed, and I found myself saying in tones of hushed surprise, "Well, I'll be damned!" In all the years of my ministry I have never had a more revealing experience of the difference between religion and a particular Religion.

The Religions are sometimes unwilling to recognize the basic universality of religious experience or to distinguish between religion and the Religions. On the contrary, they are sometimes theologically and doctrinally autocratic, anti-rational and protagonists of the status quo. An editorial, the "Authoritarian Temptation" (*Commonweal*, October 28, 1955) uttered an appropriate warning to Roman Catholics. "It seems that despite the church's profound position on human affairs, Catholics in many instances suffer from an authoritarian temptation which leads them into political traps and historic blind alleys. It leads them, for instance, into supporting dictators like Juan Peron and Francisco Franco, as long as these dictators are friends of their particular Religion. The worst scoundrel, the most oppressive tyrant can find his Catholic supporters if only he is willing to pay lip service to the church.

"The position of the church on freedom is clearly and eloquently stated. With a daring that must puzzle those who fail to understand her depth, the church has always maintained that a man must obey his conscience when he is subjectively certain that it is correct, even though in any given situation his conscience may be in error. Here is a guarantee of man's freedom that neither time nor power can corrode. Despite the failings and persecutions of history, despite the arrogance and pretentions of totalitarian regimes, despite even the intolerance and blindness of many Catholics, the freedom of the human spirit can find a sure refuge as long as the church endures."

However, one cannot escape the thought that this is a slender and unstable foundation on which to base man's freedom and his right to distinguish between religion and the Religions.

Among the orthodox of all Religions there seems to be an inclination to take dogmatic positions. One cannot help but ask: Does orthodoxy naturally breed fanaticism? Is there something inherent in the orthodox mind that naturally tends toward bigotry? Surely, though this appears to be so, it need not necessarily be so, for all orthodoxies have bred their saints.

* * *

I recognize, of course, that in all the Religions there are leaders in pulpit and pew who, while they are affiliated with a particular Religion, do not necessarily accept the official interpretation of the faith as expressed in articles, dogma or principles. Many ministers and laymen have gone beyond the prescribed limits in their thinking and ceremonial practice; it is as if there were a sacred corner of their minds where no one may enter. Family memories and ties of loyalty to an institution, concern for children's religious education, and the less praiseworthy motives of social ambition or because "it is the thing to do," and sometimes even fear hangovers from early childhood teaching, prevent the expression of convictions contrary to those for which the rabbi, minister or priest, indeed the denomination, is supposed to stand. It is impossible to determine the number of dissidents enrolled in church and synagogue, but they are many. I have no quarrel with them save to point out how much the brave and open mind is needed at this moment in history.

Which is more important: that a man shall have faith or that he shall subscribe to the beliefs which constitute the substance of *your* faith? And if the beliefs of his faith should differ from the beliefs of your faith, will you say that man is not religious? Surely this limits and shrinks religion to the dimensions of your particular faith. You are placing a mean and lower value upon the religions which encompass all mankind. Such thinking is characteristic of the closed mind!

Dr. Von Ogden Vogt, one of the distinguished elder teachers of our generation, points out in his *The Primacy of Worship* (Starr King Press, 1958), "The open mind of classicism and the searching mind of science are united in a struggle with medieval and reformation dogmatism. A deep but needless cleft between these forces is not lessening but widening. It is an ominous division, which if not healed, will bring untold disasters of spiritual disorder upon our nation and upon mankind." He proposes to give "primary place to worship which unites rather than to beliefs which divide." I can agree with his emphasis upon the things that unite rather than the things that divide, but worship unfortunately, and frequently, separates men from each other, particularly when they believe that the form of worship is as important as worship itself. They will not worship with those whose form differs from their own —for example, some Orthodox Jews, some Evangelical Protestants, and some Roman Catholics.

I believe that any Religion which says, "I have the truth and that truth is necessary to your salvation," is somewhat less than liberal. To lay such flattering unction to itself suggests a form of blasphemy. The most that any sect can say is that to us, our interpretation of the supreme being, of God, is truth. The most that I can say is that, for me, my Judaism represents the clearest expression of religious truth, one, which it is hoped, your Religion represents for you. But when any Religion sets itself up as the sole repository of truth, and declares that its truth is necessary to salvation, the open mind begins to question. For it is just such an attitude as this which has in the past led to tyranny, abuse and even murder in the name of God.

The organized Religions are, further, often anti-rationalistic. When conflicts appear between what has been held traditionally true and the discoveries of science, when the Bible says one thing and science says another, when a Religion makes the claim upon its devotees: "Give up your own thinking, do not exercise your

God-given powers of reason, believe not as your intelligence prompts you, but as I tell you"; when conformity is obtained through ecclesiastical authority—hypocrisy and a lack of intellectual integrity are often the unpleasant by-product.

The enactment of an unenforceable law makes hypocrites of our citizens. Similarly, denial of the right to think, rejection of the privilege to examine principle and dogma critically—an anti-rationalistic attitude—makes hypocrites of religionists. Men seek to avoid and contravene laws that are distasteful to them. The eighteenth amendment, for instance, not representing the opinion of millions of citizens, was ignored, violated, set at naught, and in the process created a shameful national hypocrisy and disrespect for all law.

And when men are told to believe what contradicts their reason, when the outward pressure is too great for them to break away from organized Religion, they mouth phrases, repeat formulas, and go through ceremonies in a purely perfunctory way, secretly despising themselves and the system which makes this necessary. Finally, they accustom themselves to the situation; the self-reproach disappears. But when that takes place, something has gone out of the soul of a man. He has lost his intellectual integrity. And the disintegration of his character does not end there; it moves on like a virus, infecting the whole of life and conduct. The man becomes ethically callous, socially selfish, spiritually blind. Thus, it not infrequently happens that men and women in church and synagogue, lay and clerical, actually stand in opposition to the spirit of religion.

The Religions have too often become protagonists of the *status quo*. Supported in large measure by the wealthy men of a community, they take on the prejudices of the substantial contributors. And consequently, discussion of the problems of poverty, abuses by capital or labor in the industrial order, crime, graft, and corruption, become anathema. If the minister, the priest or the rabbi dares to speak out about these things, he will be branded a controversial figure, dangerous, a Red, and he may lose his job. This has happened in innumerable instances. It occurs today. Or men say to their minister: "We come to our place of worship to find peace; we do not want to be upset or disturbed. Social, economic, and political discussions have no place in the pulpit. Talk religion!"

For these reasons many ministers are forced to walk and talk warily or be silent. The man in the pew and in the street knows the pressures exerted on the minister and sees their effect on him, in his thinking, his speaking and his conduct. The moral authority of the minister thus becomes weakened and his word discounted.

The Religions cannot ignore the maladjustments of society. True it is, there are welfare councils and social service committees in the great denominational groups, but they are often under fire and regarded as dreamers, fanatics or Reds! There are, of course, exceptions, all the more eloquent just because they are few. Such exceptions should become the rule in these days when it is so popular to label anything liberal as subversive.

If the abuses which I have described are sometimes true, then it is you and I who have failed in our basic responsibility to live the religious truths to which we have committed ourselves, to practice brotherhood with men of other faiths. If we have failed in this primary responsibility, then perhaps we have still to learn what it is that Moses and Jesus were talking about.

* * *

Let me now try to make clear the distinction between religion and the Religions by an interpretation of the nature of religion and the religious personality.

When man began to grapple intelligently with the thought of life and destiny, he naturally faced the problem of his relation to the universe and to his fellow men. The idea of God seemed necessary to such a relation, and he set out to prove God's existence as a fact. He built intricate systems of theology on a faith which often ignored or rejected the demands of reason. With the development of scientific theory and invention and the application of reason to the principles of faith, the idea of God was rejected in some quarters as unnecessary. In the field of religion, though there were many changes in interpretation, the idea of God continued to be a persistent assumption which the theologians tried to prove. It is not necessary to rehash the old arguments or to try to prove the existence of God. I do not believe it is possible by reason either to prove or to disprove the existence of God; for now, as always, the idea of God remains and must remain the basic assumption of religion. I choose rather to approach the subject pragmatically, and I trust logically, and to indicate how great an influence the idea of God may have in the life of men and women and on human relations.

On his eightieth birthday the late Alexander Steinmetz was asked what would be the unique achievement of the twentieth century. The scientist is reported to have answered that just as the nineteenth century was marked by extraordinary technological discoveries which have made life more comfortable for men and communications swift and smooth, the twentieth century would be marked by discoveries in the realm of the spirit. Man would, he believed, learn more about himself, his feelings, impulses and drives, all of which determine human conduct. With these deeper insights, Steinmetz went on to say, man will conquer himself and fashion nobler patterns of living. Surely Steinmetz is right in that we shall probably come to know much more about the mind and its strange workings and about what we call the spirit.

But an old problem presents itself—is intelligence enough? What is it that transforms intelligence into disciplined, socially useful conduct? I may know what is right to do, but I may choose to do what is wrong. Man can build an airplane, but that plane can drop bombs as well as healing drugs and plasma. Man discovered radio and television, but these can spread falsehoods and stir hate as well as truth and brotherhood. Intelligence and sometimes even knowledge are in themselves amoral. Intelligence recognizes the distinction between truth and falsehood but the difference between good and evil, right and wrong, does not come within its ken.

Of itself, intelligence is not necessarily concerned with values, and the worth of man's knowledge or intelligence must be judged by the use he makes of it. The question then becomes, to what end should men use intelligence? And the answer is, we believe, evident: Man should use his intelligence for the advancement of life. But how shall he use it? How can he be moved to use intelligence for the advancement of life? To use his knowledge or his intelligence for the advancement of life, man must have a sense of responsibility, one which is so overwhelming that everything that he knows and feels and does becomes an instrument for good.

But responsibility has to have an object. Parents are responsible for the health and education of their children. Society is responsible for the handicapped and those unable to take care of themselves. The good lawyer endeavors to maintain the highest standards of his profession. The doctor always bears in mind the Hippocratic oath. The artist, poet or musician yields homage, as does the scientist, to harmony, to wholeness, to truth, to beauty. Workers are responsible to their employers; employers to their workers, and both to the public. Leaders are responsible to those who lift them to power. Nations are responsible to the world community. Responsibility is always related to something outside itself, larger than itself, which chastens, refines, disciplines and civilizes conduct. These responsibilities are valid; they are recognized, though they may not always be accepted.

For the religious man, however, all these responsibilities have a deeper meaning. For him there is a further and more basic responsibility because of which all the others seem to take on larger meaning. For the religious man, God is the object of his supreme responsibility. Because of this, every responsibility he feels is pervaded by a drive, an impulsion of compelling power, to realize itself in its object. It colors everything he thinks and feels and does. It fills him with a sense of gratitude. It chastens his joys and mitigates his sorrows. It urges him to courtesy, consideration and kindness. It is his constant companion. It prompts him to usefulness. It is the most persistent motivation of his life, relating him and his labors to the fullness of the universe, as the segment of a circle reaches from circumference to center, and without this segment the circle would be incomplete. It blesses him with a serenity no storm can disturb. For the religious man, the idea of God and the sense of responsibility to him are indeed a transforming experience. For the individual it means the cultivation of every capacity and the direction of it to the common good. It means the constant disciplining of prejudices. It means an effort to appreciate differences of race, creed, culture and religion, and the consequent respect for each. It means the development of the international mind. It marks the difference between a man who happens to live in the twentieth century and a civilized human being.

What a change would take place in the world if, in his bungling and confusion, man could find the object of his responsibility in the idea of God. The little things would assume a greater responsibility, and the things we take so much for granted would be hallowed by the radiance of eternity. Children would be drawn closer to parents and parents to children and the home would become a sanctuary. Our labors of body and mind would become part of an infinite striving for fulfillment and completion.

The distinction between religion and the Religions now becomes clear. Religion speaks of a supreme being; the Religions declare a supreme being to be one or two or three or many. Religion declares God has revealed himself through the ages; the Religions declare that God revealed himself in a particular place, a particular time—in India, at Sinai, at Bethlehem or Mecca, and through a specific individual or group. Religion proclaims that all the prophets of all peoples glimpsed something of the supreme being; the Religions affirm that primarily or only through Buddha, Moses, Jesus, Mohammed, the Bishop of Rome, Coué, or Mary Baker Eddy, did the supreme being reveal himself.

This distinction between the Religions must be acknowledged, not only in order to think clearly, but to avoid misunderstanding. Such a distinction is natural; it rises out of the normal differences among men; it is historically understandable, and appears to be rationally justified. One of the first duties of the thoughtful person then is to make the distinction clear. My Religion, your Religion, these are one thing; but religion is another thing.

CHAPTER FOUR

Reason Is As Important As Faith

Heartily know,
When half-gods go,
The Gods arrive.

R. W. EMERSON

Reason is as important as faith and man must
have companionship with both, if he would keep the
windows of revelation open.

Reason is the great corrector. To its awesome
critique we must be ready to submit our deepest con-
victions, so that all that is irrational, erroneous and
superstitious may be laid aside, and the larger truth
revealed.

I S there a revival of religion today? Many claim there is. Boxers
dropping to their knees just before the bell and crossing themselves, and television masters of ceremonies liberally introducing
into their program a "God bless you, dear lady" to some size 44
female who smiles dreamily as she accepts flowers or perfume, seem
artificial to me, and in exceedingly bad taste. But more seriously,
the popularity of books like the late Rabbi Joshua Liebman's
Peace of Mind, Bishop Sheen's *Peace of Soul*, and Dr. Norman
Vincent Peale's *The Power of Positive Thinking* would seem to

confirm it. The enthusiastic crowds which attend Billy Graham's meetings apparently strengthen the claim. And the widespread interest among college students in courses in religion would appear to offer final proof that we are witnessing a religious revival of extraordinary proportions. The answers to this question depend on what we mean by revival and what one means by religion.

The same assertion was made after World War I. A spate of books on spiritualism appeared. Anguished hearts refused to accept death as utterly final. People naturally turned to hope in life after death. The uncertain, troubled years between the great wars, with the resurgence of hate-movements, growing tensions between capital and labor, between the races and nations and the final catastrophe of 1939-45 hardly indicated there had been a revival of religion. Whatever greater interest there is in religion today is probably testimony to man's bewilderment, his longing for security in a world whose tomorrow no one can predict. It may be what Arnold Toynbee calls the "touch of adversity" which has made us more thoughtful.

Progress seems to have been but a fond illusion; international cooperation, a vanishing mirage. The very worth and value of the democratic process is questioned. Man stands before the atomic age with the fire of heaven in his hands but he does not know how he will use it.

Hesitant and faltering, frightened at the new power he has discovered, exhausted by the contrary and warring impulses in his own spirit, he seems to feel the need for some help, some source of strength other than that which he possesses within himself.

The Religions appear to offer the assurance which will mitigate his dilemma, and so many convert and return to the old altars.

In my youth I remember revival meetings held by Gypsy Smith under a tent in the Park Extension in Savannah, Georgia. I was hardly old enough to apply the canons of critical reason to what he said, but the magic of his voice, the impression of his sincerity, tugged at the very depths of my being, though I was revolted by the convulsion "fits" of some of the men and women who pro-

claimed their newborn faith. I remember also the revivals of Sam
Jones and especially the meetings of Billy Sunday, after whose
muscular evangelical efforts, many "hit the sawdust trail."

Billy Graham conducted a series of revival meetings in Paris in
the Palais des Sports several years ago. I was eager to hear this
young man whose influence is so profound that even the dignified
Church of England and the Lutheran Church on the continent
and in Scandinavia have cooperated in his efforts. The Palais de
Sports was two-thirds full with 12,000 people, not a meager congregation of Protestants in a nominally Catholic land. I went in
reverence. I came away sad. I had hoped to hear some vibrant word,
some new approach to the religious life. I heard an apparently
dedicated and attractive young man speaking in the familiar vocabulary of traditional theology and with an obvious sincerity that at
least did credit to his personal integrity. It was an eminently re-
spectable performance. A sort of proper Victorian restraint marked
the proceedings.

Two years later I heard Graham again during his New York
crusade. Although the meetings had been going on for over two
months, the vast arena of Madison Square Garden was completely
filled. Subtle yet definable changes had taken place since the Paris
meeting. American advertising, organization and propaganda
methods had come into the picture. Graham's theology was the
same: "I give you God through Jesus and Him crucified." But
here was a show, a good show with all the techniques of the theater
—lighting, the youth who testified—while Graham, a new Graham,
not the calm Graham of the Paris meetings, but a man seemingly
possessed, who spoke with passion and flailing arms and waited as
the massed choir sang softly.

Some hundreds stood at his feet that night. But once again I
was sad for them and for the world. Here was mass emotion
expertly exploited, for critical intelligence had fled this hall and
passive acceptance had taken its place.

I listened to the conversation of people as they walked out of
the meeting. I wondered if all the excitement and the statement

"the crusade is the talk of the town" indicated that to go to hear the evangelist was not just another "one of the things to do" in New York. It was said that over 50,000 "decisions" were made during the crusade. I wondered how many were repeaters. One minister of a large church on Park Avenue stated that during the period of the Garden meetings, three cards had been sent him by the Graham organization, signed by people who had attended the revival. "Two had been members of my church for many years and the third was a 'nut'." I wondered how many of the so-called new conversions would last. I wondered if the "crusade" would backfire and if those who had been told with such certainty "tomorrow you will wake to a new life" would be disillusioned when they faced the same problems as before. I wondered if in the end all the time and money and energy would have been worth-while. I don't know! I hope some good was accomplished and that the "crusade" will not prove to have been just a "flash in the pan." But as I passed out of the atmosphere of Madison Square Garden into the streets crowded with New Yorkers, visitors in town and eager-eyed youth on the prowl, I wondered if the excited, throbbing, impersonal, hard-working, pleasure-seeking spirit of the great metropolis had really been touched.

I do not doubt that there are "conversions" in the traditional sense of the word which transform life — for instance, Wesley's moving description of the "strange warming" of his heart which he felt at that meeting in London after which he went forth to found the great Methodist movement; or, for instance, Paul Claudel's account of that moment in Notre Dame after which he was a different man. But conversions often make fanatics of the convert. Indeed Claudel became an uncompromising devotee, often bitterly impatient of contrary opinion; and certainly it can hardly be said that G. K. Chesterton and Hilaire Belloc were filled with sweetness and light. The same might be said of some converted Protestants. It surely can be said of many Jews whose lives for the first time have been touched by the emotionalism of mass Jewish feeling. Any unbiased judgment must state that such conversions are not so much to religion as to a particular Religion. Any religious revival to be sound must be enduring, must manifest itself in changed lives, in more just and brotherly conduct, must rid itself of the fury of fanaticism; must have some basis in rationality.

In a sense what some call a revival of religion is one manifestation of the contemporary tendency to run with the crowd, to belong, to be like everyone else, do what everyone else is doing, dress like everyone else, see the same plays and motion pictures, and read the same books that everyone else is reading. The cult of conformity! The fear of being different. It began with the mass production of clothing and proceeded to mass production in education. Pressures for conformity were heightened by the media of communication—radio and television. They became more insistent as the uncertainties of life were made more obvious in a world where aggressive, imperialist Communism bars no holds. These pressures for conformity now impinge on the field of the Religions.

There is a difference between religious revival as we much too loosely call it and yearning for religion. I believe there is a yearning for religion today which may lead to religious revival. That this is true is evidenced on our college campuses. The increased enrollment in religious courses and discussion groups has not led to any measurable increase in chapel attendance when such attendance is voluntary or in denominational affiliation.

Youth is disturbed by the distance between what we profess and what we practice. We voice morals and fail to live up to them. We speak of peace and prepare for war. We declare our devotion to the teachings of Christianity and Judaism, but betray that devotion in our daily conduct. All about them young people see confusion and drift as well as the selfishness of individuals and groups. They feel their present is insecure and their future uncertain. My own conclusions after years of college preaching and innumerable "bull sessions" on many campuses confirm the conclusions of Stanley Rowland, Jr., who, in a recent article in the *New York Times* wrote, "There is not so much a religious revival as there is a religious search."

We may not discount the yearning and the search. They are not limited to idealistic youth. And the "angry young men" or "beat generation" are but expressing in drama and novel not only their indignation at things as they are, but their frustration as they see the gaping chasm between their dreams and the mad world we, their fathers, have bequeathed them. The yearning and the search are real. How often men and women have come to me and said, "I wish I could believe, I want to believe, tell me how to believe. I want some anchor in our apparently endlessly drifting world. I want to believe that somehow somewhere in all this persistent change there is that which endures. I want to believe that all I dream of truth and beauty and goodness are somehow underwritten in the scheme of things." I tell them, "I cannot give you faith. Keep the heart open, let the mind follow the heart's lead, while disciplining its enthusiasms with reason. Go out under the stars at night and look up at the myriads of worlds beyond our present ken. Do not turn away frustrated because of what you cannot comprehend. Perhaps the beauty and the wonder will bring you serenity. Or ponder the mysteries of your own being. Seek with whatever geiger counters you have of sensitivity; search in music, in art, in literature, in the goodness of men. It may be that some divine spirit is trying to break through to you."

Yearning and searching are not confined to any one religious group. They are much more profound than "conversion" in the accepted sense of the word. They have something to do with acceptance of old truths and joining a church or synagogue. They have very much more to do with a reappraisal of our religious beliefs.

For the faithful and active Roman Catholic, perhaps, there is no hesitation, no questioning doubt, no critical re-examination of his faith. What he is told to believe and what he believes are not only the substance of truth as revealed in the dogma of the church but the means and methods of salvation, through the sacraments of the church and its hierarchical system, derived from Jesus, descending through the Bishop of Rome and from him to every regularly ordained priest. The church and Roman Catholics, of course, realize that God reveals His truth and His will for man in increasing measure; new dogmas are added and changes in practice take place as man understands more of the divine mind and will and as he grows in knowledge and grace. But any changes that do take place are enunciated through the voice of the Pope, whose declarations are infallible in matters of faith and dogma and must be accepted as the word and will of God. The church, one and indivisible, is the repository of religious truth, and proceeds in majestic dignity as the responsible instrument of God, declaring His message of redemption, waiting for the day when all mankind will be embraced in its benevolent arms and will be obedient to its laws. "There shall be but one flock and one shepherd" in the kingdom of God on earth. The pious Roman Catholic accepts these things as a matter of course. He does not question their validity. There can be no argument with him on matters of Roman Catholic faith and dogma.

Much the same spirit obtains in orthodox Evangelical Protestant Christianity and in orthodox Judaism; indeed, this spirit is found in all orthodox Religions. It seems to be an inevitable characteristic of the orthodox mind. This makes the paths of cooperation and reconciliation hard. Minds less constrained reject it. But they must learn to understand it, to live with it, and, so far as possible, work with it. Religious liberals, on the other hand, are never released from their obligation as liberals to examine their Religions constantly and persistently, in the light of contemporary knowledge; to see if their Religions promote social justice and human brotherhood in a world that cherishes freedom and is struggling toward democracy.

Postwar Protestant Christendom is stirring to what is not yet, but what might be, the greatest religious revival since the Reformation. A number of movements are clearly discernible. While they started before the war, the war brought them into sharp focus, justified them, and gave them impetus as well as direction. These movements naturally derived from the questions which earnest minds were asking. Why is organized Religion not more effective in civilizing the human race, in helping it control the brute in man, in promoting righteousness and brotherhood? Why has it not been more successful in preventing war? What is the relation of the church to society and the state? What is the nature and where is the seat of authority in faith and government? How can organized religion claim the unreserved devotion of men and give them will to realize religious ideals in their personal life and in national and international relations? Before the current upthrust of brutality and totalitarianism, which threatens all religious life and the destruction of human liberty and freedom of conscience, how can the ideals of the Protestant Reformation be maintained, promoted and extended? Such penetrating questions as these have led to an earnest re-examination of the bases of the Protestant Christian faith, its doctrines, its practices, its function. They have led also to a movement for ecumenicity, or world unity, among Protestant Christians.

It is, of course, true that some groups are hesitant about relinquishing claims to theological priority, but the world conferences of Protestants held in England, on the Continent and in the United States, before and since the war, have given striking witness to the growing power of the movement for world-wide Protestant unity. This movement is much more than a reaction to aggressive "Catholic Action." Many leaders of Protestant Christianity, faced with the vast problems of world economic reconstruction and reorganization through international cooperation, and world redemption through moral regeneration, have come to believe that only by pooling the spiritual power of its forces and directing them to such goals, can human relations be saved from chaos and man from utter despair. Nevertheless, some Protestant groups still keep aloof from the ecumenical movement.

For instance, at the recent Evanston assembly of the World Council, Bishop Berggrav advocated a common service of Communion. But the present primate of Norway told a theological conference at Northfield, Minnesota, that he and other Lutheran clergy in Norway could not approve as long as "there are different concepts of biblical truth and of the nature of the sacrament."

Organizational, denominational and personal jealousies, fear of loss of identity or relinquishment of cherished traditional practices, the weakening of a specific theological position considered to be true, social snobbishness, shortsightedness, prejudice, religious fanaticism and even bigotry—these are formidable obstacles to Protestant unity. World unity among Protestants, as I understand it, does not contemplate organic unity of the churches—that is, the disappearance of denominational groups each of which has a proud history and tradition—but rather that all liberal Christian forces of the world, united in the dynamic of Jesus' dream, shall move forward together toward attainment of God's Kingdom on earth. But the tide of the ecumenical spirit flows on and rises on the shores of many lands. It recognizes the differences among Protestants, yet insists that each may be loyal to his own denomination, and respecting all others, may and should unite in the spirit of Jesus for the redemption of the world.

An exciting development and what may well come to be one of the most important events in Christendom since the Reformation was Pope John XXIII's announcement in Rome January 25th last that he plans to call an Ecumenical Council "in order to meet the present needs of Christian peoples. . . . The convocation of the ecumenical council, in the thoughts of the Holy Father, aims not only at the edification of Christian peoples, but is intended also as an invitation to the separated communities in quest of unity. To which end so many hearts aspire in so many parts of the earth." (From the text of the Vatican Statement, New York Times, January 26, 1959.)

Before a gathering of prelates in Rome, January 29th, 1959, Pope John is reported (New York Times, January 30, 1959) to have remarked, "Let us get together with our separated brethren and let us avoid pedantic bickering about who in history was right and who was wrong. All sides may have been responsible for divisions in Christianity." However, Vatican sources consulted made it clear that "the Vatican was expecting the Eastern Christians and Protestants to 'return to the common home'—that is, to recognize the primacy of the Pope. The ecumenical council would examine ways to make such a return easier, these sources explained. They said the church could not renounce its dogma because they are held to have been defined by divine inspiration, but it could introduce changes in canon law, liturgy and church discipline. Among precedents mentioned was that of the late Pope Pius XII in waiving the rule for celibacy for married German Lutheran pastors who had embraced the Roman Catholic creed and were allowed to continue in the ministry. It was pointed out that Pope John has in no way abandoned his claim to be the chief shepherd: "There shall be but one flock and one shepherd."

Protestant reaction indicated the deep and sincere desire for Christian unity but not at the expense of the fundamental Protestant position. The idea was phrased in different ways but the meaning is the same. The invitation must not be, "You come and accept our doctrines," but rather, "Come and let us discuss our doctrines." And "the Ecumenical Council must embody two-way conversations among equals." However, the first encyclical issued by Pope John on July 2, 1959, seems to confirm Protestant reservations, for the ruler of the Roman church left no doubt that reunion meant to him the return of non-Catholics to the church.

The most serious obstacles to Christian unity seem to be the Roman Church's dogma, enunciated at the last Ecumenical Council in 1869, of the infallibility of the Pope when he speaks on faith and morals. Also Pope John's doctrinal statement stressing the cult of the Virgin Mary: "Adoration of Jesus the Saviour is at the center of any form of devotion for His Blessed Mother. . . . it is through Mary that one goes to Jesus." (*New York Times,* February 16, 1959). This doctrinal statement on Marianism was cited by many Protestant spokesmen as another major obstacle to understanding with Roman Catholics. It has been noted also that Roman Catholics have never participated in the Ecumenical Councils promoted by the Protestant World Council of Churches.

It is too much to expect organic unity of all Christians under the Bishop of Rome, but all religious and non-Christian people should hope and pray that the Ecumenical Council will be held, and that more intimate and effective techniques of cooperation between the branches of Christendom may be achieved and the moral and spiritual forces of the world strengthened.

* * *

Jews, too, are increasingly troubled by questions about human life and destiny. Though Jews have been asking these questions since Bible times, World War II has given them sharper point, deeper thrust. They are philosophic and religious questions that strike at the root of all religion.

How can we reconcile a just and merciful God with the world of injustice and war? What is the meaning of the dark ironies of existence, the Titanic forces working against each other, canceling each other out? As John Masefield put it, in his poem, "Watching By a Sick Bed," where the husband gazes upon his wife fighting for her life as he looks out the window at the sea whose billows beat upon the unyielding shore: "Why should such force fight such strength?" If God is one, is not His universe one and humanity one? Personal, moving, human questions: If God is Father, let Him show me His love. If He is merciful, where is His mercy in the world? Who can have lived these latter years and not cried out: "Oh, that He would show me some good!" Jews are asking: What is the purpose of man on earth and what is man's relation to God? How can man know God's will and how shall man yield to that will? What is the duty of man? What is the place of Israel? What is the function of Judaism? Jews are asking all the shaking questions that deal with divine and human authority and the relation between church and state, with human responsibility, with economic and social justice, international organization, war and peace. Doubt and cynicism are no more general among Jews than among Christians; but, for Jews, past and present history gives these questions greater poignancy.

If he is a believer, the Jew finds himself driven back to the simple imperatives of the mother faith. It is hard to express, organize and develop such basic ideas within the framework of a systematic theology, for they have their origin in man's search for law and order in the universe and in his desperate need to fit his beliefs about goodness and God into a world which seems to deny them.

God is. God is one. He is our Father, He is spirit. He is just, loving, eternal and omnipotent. Man is a child of God and all the people on earth are God's children to whom he is near if they call upon him. There are no theologies rooted in ancient myths claiming the renunciation of reason or the monopoly of salvation for the Jew. Only the childlike faith which prompts a man to say as he looks out on the world: Where I cannot understand, I believe; I know that God is and that my life is of worth in the vast scheme of things and that all moves toward some divine purpose. It is my duty to identify my conduct with that purpose so far as it is given to me to know it, that in the end, through me and others like me of all kinds and creeds, that purpose will be realized in God's Kingdom, not in heaven but here on earth among men and nations. I have been taught these simple and deeply true things. My fathers lived by them and died for them and so shall I.

This is the heart of Judaism. For me, this is religion with a small "r." It is the religion which Jesus learned in the synagogues of ancient Palestine. It is Judaism, the religion universal, confirmed by the eyes of man as he beholds the beauty and glory of the world, by the mind of man as he increasingly penetrates the mysteries of the universe and the laws which hold the constellations in their courses, by the heart of man as he understands the sublimity of sacrifice and love, and by the will of man as he shares in the gladness of cooperative effort.

But this Judaism through the centuries, like all Religions, has been variously interpreted. Paul interpreted it, added other elements after his own genius, and founded Christianity. Mohammed interpreted it, made his own contribution and founded the Religion of the Moslem. Jews interpreted it, their own Judaism, and the denominational groups within Judaism resulted, varying in form and ceremony, differing in attitude toward the Bible, the authority of the rabbis and the past.

Religious groups within American Jewry are beginning the arduous task of self-criticism, re-examining their traditional beliefs and practice. Storms of controversy, high winds of heated debate have already brought clear, fresh air into some of the darkened places, but the religious weather is unsettled and will continue so, one might confidently predict, for some time. Discussion centers for the most part not on the simple truths which are matters of faith and cannot be proved but rather on the interpretation, expression and fulfillment of these truths within traditional patterns.

Just as the Protestant world is striving toward unity, so in the Jewish world there is a movement toward unity. The desire for unity among Jews today naturally grows out of the position of the Jews in the world. It has a philosophic and, to some extent, a theological basis. In this it parallels the desire for unity among Protestants and Catholics; but perhaps its primary motive is a frantic search for survival not only for the Jew as an individual but for Jews as a people. The most compelling and powerful expression of the desire for unity and survival is Jewish nationalism or Zionism. The Zionist controversy cuts across every area of Jewish thinking and endeavor. It is manifest in the religious divisions of American Judaism; it shows itself in the relief, welfare and social organization of Jews; and, unfortunately, it has recently moved into the field of American politics in places where there are a large number of Jews.

The only possible basis for American Jewish unity, the only basis compatible with the spirit of America, is religio-cultural. We are joiners and supporters of this, that and the other cause, Jewish and general, like our neighbors. American Jews should not and dare not unite as Jews for the promotion of Jewish nationalist or Zionist political aims either here or abroad. We want no Jewish imperium within an American imperium. Such a step would attack the very foundations of the American tradition of the separation of church and state. We have criticized similar efforts in other groups. What is wrong for them is not right for us.

Meanwhile, surveys are being conducted, studies being made, tentative programs initiated which reveal the complexity and difficulties of the problem of Jewish unity. The Jews of America have begun the therapeutic exercise of self-examination. They have not yet accepted the healing therapy of earnest self-criticism. Like the Protestant community, the Jewish community is busily engaged in earnest self-criticism, moves slowly and laboriously toward the realization of its deeply rooted anxiety for unity within its own ranks and some expression of its identification with the world Jewish community consonant with Jewish tradition and the American scene.

This current Christian-Jewish examination of basic ideas is cleansing and healthy. It represents the introduction of reason into the problems of the organized Religions and recognition of the importance of reason in relation to matters of theology as well as in the practical concerns of institutionalized religion.

* * *

There are other tendencies, influences, and movements among the Religions which are neither cleansing nor wholesome. In a sense they represent a revolt against reason. It is true they rise out of the urgencies of our time, out of the very processes of self-examination in which the liberal Religions are engaged, but I regard them with apprehension because they minimize the proper function of reason in relation to faith, because they deepen the consciousness of difference rather than encourage the will to cooperation. *They make for dissension not harmony. They promote the primacy of the Religious group which is particularistic, rather than the religious idea which is universal.*

What are these tendencies? They are, in general, a retreat to authority, and an assumption of sovereignty in areas, which in a democracy, belong to the state. These influences are at work in large or small degree in Roman Catholicism, in Protestant Christianity and in Judaism. Let us examine them briefly to inquire whether they further the fulfillment of the universal in all the Religions or whether they retard it; whether they unite men in fellowship or whether they separate them; whether they build bridges or whether they build walls.

* * *

Man needs authority and therefore he will seek it constantly. He is so framed that he must yield loyalty to that which is greater than he. Sometimes man finds the authority he seeks in the emotions, sometimes in the intellect. All our political forms, economic systems, social institutions, and religious patterns resulted from man's recognition of the need for some authority and reflect the sovereignty of both faith and reason. But history also reveals an apparent struggle between the emotional and the rational for the dominance of man's life. The eighteenth century was marked by a revolt against the authority of uncritical faith and by the elevation of reason.

In our day a counter-movement can be sensed: a revolt against reason and a retreat to authority. It manifests itself not only in the areas of politics and economics, but also in the field of religion. We question the achievements of the liberating forces of the last two centuries. We have become afraid of the things that we have built. We fear the directions in which we move. We fear our very visions and dreams. In the face of fear, men often act as animals do—they seek their burrows. And human beings, in the midst of a period of uncertainty and doubt, when there is a flaming interrogation point in the pentecostal skies, dig back to their origins. It takes stamina to face forward and seek the new day, especially when the sun is clouded over and the storms beat about our heads.

We are bewildered before the rising power of the contemporary revolutionary movements. We are told that democracy is weak and decadent, that it is outmoded as a political system. We are told that our economic system has committed suicide. We are told that our religious heritage is a delusion. We yearn for stability, security, and certainty. We are offered the unhappy stability of regimentation, the uneasy security of dictatorship, and the alleged certainties of faith in the leader, the party, the race or the church.

The old questions of God's existence and the destiny of man on earth force themselves upon us. Inscrutable mysteries surround us, and we seem to be the victims of blind, insensate forces that have little regard for our welfare or happiness. We seek the answers and find them not. Yet we need to anchor our lives to some great conviction; we need to find some authority that compels obedience from our restless spirit, one that will bring it serenity and some measure of joy. And so some turn to the surrogate of an uncritical, authoritarian faith. This tendency is manifest among Jews and Christians.

One of the most disarming and subtly dangerous retreats to authority is that which is offered the Christian world in the philosophy of St. Thomas Aquinas. Neo-Thomism is a valiant and needed protest against the confusion of the times which appeals to many as a way out. But its claims must be examined with care.

A distinguished interpreter of the Neo-Thomist position, Professor Anton Pegis of the Medieval Institute in Toronto, states the issue this way: "In our anxiety to be tolerant with each other and of each other's right to live according to the dictates of his own conscience, we have unthinkingly fostered the habit of tolerance in relation to truth itself. . . . Wrong convictions can lead us to disaster." But the uninitiated naturally asks the old embarrassing question: "What is truth?" And the answer is: "Oh, ours, of course."

The Neo-Thomist goes back to the thirteenth century because he believes that at that time, as in ours, man was facing the same problem he faces today—the quest of his own dignity, the need to find some unity in the madly clashing discords of nature and human life; the quest for an authority that guarantees them. Man's dignity and the unity of all things derive from God, as do man's freedom, his right to work, his security, his leisure, and his happiness. So far so good. But the Neo-Thomist rejects the free, the open mind. Because a mind is free it is hardly fair to call it irrational. Is it irrational to speak of growth, unfolding? They are the heart of the educational process. To recognize this indicates humility. And humility is still a grace, wherever it is found. It can hardly be said to have its habitation where men speak with such complete finality about the great truths toward which we all grope our faltering way.

A distinguished protagonist of the Thomistic School, Professor Jacques Maritain, Princeton Institute for Advanced Study, in a brilliant address at the University of Pennsylvania on "Contemporary Renewals in Religious Thought," referred to the inner tensions which the religious philosophy of Dr. Karl Barth reflects. He says Dr. Barth "would seem to be anxiously questioning himself and continually wondering whether this ardent word which is so stimulating to his followers, and his renewed Protestant theology, is the word of Karl Barth or the word of God." But the Neo-Thomists have no doubt that *their* interpretations are the word of God. At least Dr. Barth at the moment has the grace of humility which in some quarters is still deemed the essence of religion.

With profound respect for its sincerity, I suggest that the Neo-Thomists' claim that their position reinstates and elevates the authority of reason is unwarranted. Rather, it is a retreat to authority which rejects reason.

The Rev. Bernard E. Gilgun in discussing Christian culture from the point of view of Neo-Thomism declared in a letter to *Commonweal*, May 20, 1955, "Our starting point must be an intelligent and consequential *act of Faith* [italics ours] in doctrines of the Creation, Fall and Redemption of man. And that is not at all the same thing as 'religion' or 'worship.'" As a Thomist he takes the position that St. Thomas "unlike the manualists of our day, made no apology for treating the theology as a bona fide science, as distinct from Faith as chemistry is from mathematics."

It is possible to erect a logically sound structure based on certain premises. This is what Professor William F. Albright of Johns Hopkins University does in his recent volume, *Return to Biblical Theology*. He asserts that he is moved by a dedication to scientific method, that the discipline of reason is basic in his approach to Biblical literature; and yet he appeals for a return to the theology of the patriarchs. This is but another form of worship of the word. This is also what the Thomists do. They exercise reason *only after certain things are granted*. And it is just these things—and they are by no means unimportant—that the free intelligence will not grant. To ascribe the attribute of rationality to a theological schematism which demands an act of uncritical acceptance from the very start is to deal with words as the totalitarians deal. For instance, the Thomist distinction between natural law and divine law is plausible, but it serves the purpose of denominational dialectics rather than universal truth. The free intelligence must beware of the dogma which insists that its definition of divine law is truth. Grant the premise and the dialectician will lead you along a path whose end is an intellectual and spiritual authoritarianism.

I am reminded of the story told by the late Dr. David Philipson of Cincinnati, Ohio, a leading Reform rabbi. He had invited a number of literary men to meet the late Israel Zangwill, one of the most distinguished English writers of his day. Among them was a certain Mr. Good. Mr. Good considered himself to be a philosopher, but he was very obscure in his thought and expression. He engaged Zangwill in an argument on the new psychology, and as usual, was quite obscure. After listening to him for a few moments, Zangwill said, "Mr. Good, you misunderstand yourself!"

One of the most eloquent Protestant expressions of a similar retreat to authority in the area of religion is a widely read essay by Mr. T.S. Eliot, *The Idea of a Christian Society*. The Christian state, apart from any sectarian dogmatics, *ideally* would be the Jewish state, and it would be the Muslim state. I am not interested in labels. I do fear a philosophy of life that rejects the intellectual processes, that denies to man the right to exercise his intelligence and retreats to a religious authoritarianism.

Mr. Eliot pleads for *one authority* in his ideal state. After an incisive analysis of our times and a bitter and moving criticism of it—our drifting, our lack of standards, our rejection of values—he throws up his hands in despair and declares there must be some authority, and that that authority must be religious. His solution of our present ills is a state religion, a theocratic state. But that is an archaic idea. Centuries ago, a large part of the Christian world revolted against the theocratic state. Reason and experience combined to evolve what most of us today believe to be a better way. Mr. Eliot and those who share this point of view appeal to us to move forward—to the past!

One may well ask the practical question—was the level of society any higher in mediaeval times than it is today? Beneath the outward peace and social order of the mediaeval period we hear so often glorified today, beneath all the artistic monuments to the creative genius of the human spirit, we see vassalage and cruelty and the bloody Crusades. It was an age of political irresponsibility, an age of unreason, an age of darkness. The period that followed was rightly labelled the Renaissance.

Furthermore, we have a number of examples of the theocratic state in our contemporary world. Is the intellectual level of the people of Spain or Italy or certain Latin American countries any higher than that of the people in the United States? Are standards of personal conduct higher, are human relations any more just? We may ask the same questions concerning the people of certain countries where Protestantism is the established Religion or concerning the people of Israel where orthodox Judaism is the established religion.

I find myself baffled by such thinking. It asserts it is objectively rational, yet it is devious, casuistic; it is reason exalting itself! There is something decadent about it. In politics it leads to authoritarianism; in literature it produces the cult of brittle cleverness, the quip for itself. It is the decadence of a man who considers himself at the center of life, or one who seeks peace in departure from the world.

I have referred at some length to Neo-Thomism as it manifests itself in Roman Catholicism and Protestantism, because it is somewhat in vogue and proclaimed loud, long, subtly, and persistently. A general acceptance of such a point of view and its application to modern life would mean a rejection of reason, a return to the authority of blind faith, a restoration of the union between church and state, and the ultimate destruction of our democratic society. The inevitable result of Thomist thinking is the theocratic state.

Philosophies of life express themselves in feeling and conduct. A people acts and molds its laws and customs on the basis of what it believes and feels. The authority the neo-mediaevalists, Jewish and Christian, offer us is no solution for the contemporary religious, moral or economic crisis. It was tried and rejected. The somewhat obscure light that shines from these mediaeval towers cannot dull the brilliance that still shines from Sinai and the Mount of Olives!

Recently in Paris, a distinguished French Roman Catholic layman asked me, "Why don't you become a Roman Catholic?" He continued, "My close friend, the late Henri Bergson toward the end of his life was strongly drawn to the Roman Church, even though he never actually converted, because the Nazi persecutions of the Jew awakened something in him which prevented the step. But the essential mysticism in his philosophy found kinship with the mysticism of the Church and he felt himself being driven spiritually and intellectually toward Rome because of its historic background, its universality and because it is the logical development of Judaism as well as its fulfillment."

I replied that there is a mysticism in Judaism, not only in the Psalms, but in rabbinical philosophy; that so far as historic background is concerned, Judaism is centuries older; that the insights of Judaism are equally universal; and that what he called the "logical development of Judaism" in Roman Catholicism, is not really a logical development and fulfillment, but a turn-off from the main stream of Judaism into a theological by-path whose claims to authority cannot be justified by reason.

Certainly Protestant Christianity cannot ignore or reject that idea which is the very essence of its being—the right of the individual conscience to interpret truth and life and God and man's relation to God and his fellow man. No theological system, however weighted with scholarly documentation, starting with certain accepted yet not-to-be-criticized premises, can take the place of the traditional Protestant insistence upon the worth and dignity of the questing mind. Protestant thinkers—if I may humbly and most reverently suggest—must beware the bewitchments of a return to mediaeval thinking, no matter how appealingly expressed or how packed with powerful and often overwhelming verbiage. These questions should be asked: What premises are they asked to accept? Can these premises stand the critique of reason or do they reject it? Where do these premises lead? What will be their practical application in human relations? The contemporary Protestant search for authority need not reject the claims of reason. Religious authority in Protestantism, if I understand it, as in Judaism, has been subject always to the free critical intelligence.

One example of the retreat to authority is the assault upon the principle of free, liberal, public education. The attack is dangerous because it often cloaks itself in the garb of religion. Education is so liberal, it is charged that it has no basic values. It is irrational and therefore glorifies futility. The basis of much of the present criticism of American education is a retreat to an authoritarianism which is no less dangerous to democracy because it speaks in the name of religion; no less dangerous than the authoritarianism which expresses itself in economics or politics. Diatribes against our educational philosophy, system, and methods are nothing new.

The vicious condemnation of such educational liberals as Professor William Kilpatrick and the late John Dewey by some Catholic, Protestant and Jewish educators are cases in point. These trailblazers of a better order of society are charged with disseminating educational doctrines and theories "incompatible with the fundamental tenets on which American liberties are founded." The charges, of course, are not true. Indeed, it should be pointed out that the entire burden of John Dewey's *Freedom and Culture* is the recognition of moral values in man and the universe and the task of man, according to Dewey, is the release and fulfillment of these values in the personal life and in human relations and institutions. I shall never forget the hours I spent some years ago in conversation with Professor Kilpatrick at Williamstown. They were profoundly religious experiences.

I deeply respect the religious convictions of all men. I should like to see our educational system filled with teachers who, in interpreting the facts of life, give place to that sense of mystery, wonder, and miracle, as well as that consciousness of responsibility to God and man, which are at the heart of religion. I believe this can be achieved by the joint effort of religious groups working with educational specialists; and I believe the nation would benefit and the substance of our curricula would be enriched without intrusion upon sectarian religious biases.

Dissatisfaction with our failures in the field of education, however, should not move us to blame the system of free, liberal, public school education for our national shortcomings and cause us to favor state-supported denominational schools.

One might ask with all candor and with no reflection upon any group—for there are Protestant and, to some extent, Jewish* as well as Catholic parochial schools—do crime and criminal statistics reflect a smaller degree of law-breakers among those groups who do not share in our system of public education than among those whose children attend the public schools?

An authoritative study of a cross-section of the prison and reformatory population would surely reveal whether the products of denominational or parochial school education are less criminally inclined than those of our public schools. Such an objective study has been made and its results give us some definite data on which

* It is interesting to note that in a report given to the annual convention of Religious Zionists, held in Atlantic City November, 1958, by Rev. Dr. Isidor Margolis, Executive Director of the Torah Education Council, it was revealed that in the last ten years the Jewish day school system had increased its schools from 20 to 260, its pupils from 2,000 to 40,000, and its annual budget from $6,000,000 to $30,000,000.

to base a more accurate appraisal of the effectiveness of our educational system.

An advisory opinion of the New York State probation commission in the recent controversy over probation officers reported that of 10,899 new cases filed in the courts in 1954, fifty per cent were Roman Catholic, forty-five per cent were Protestant and five per cent were Jewish. It is somewhat presumptuous to suggest that our public schools have failed. Perhaps the failure lies elsewhere.

None of this must be taken as a defense of present conditions. There is much to criticize and much to be bettered. Nor does anything I have said minimize the value I place upon the worth and function of the Religions. I hope merely to clarify an issue which may confuse the well-meaning and well-intentioned and prompt them in their anxiety to "do something about it," to support programs which, if carried to their logical conclusion, might well break down the American principle of separation of church and state, open the way for the abandonment of our public school system and the setting up in its place of denominationally supported schools.

* * *

Coincident with the disinclination to apply the disciplines of reason to religious faith and deriving from the contemporary retreat to authority, I find a tendency on the part of the Religions to intrude on those areas of sovereignty which, in a democratic society, have been relegated to the state.

James Bryce, in his *American Commonwealth*, declared, "Half the wars of Europe, half the internal troubles that have vexed the European states have arisen from theological differences, or from the rival claims of church and state." Today the intrusions of the Religions on the sovereignty of the state have resulted in clericalism and anti-clericalism and create deep schisms among the citizens of Germany (Bavaria), Italy, France, Holland, and Belgium.

Union of church and state is one of the basic causes of the

smoldering dissension and strife between what was Old India and the Succession States. In Israel, the government fell some time ago because of the insistence of the Religious bloc that it be given control of education, marriage and divorce. The question of theocracy, the union of church and state, or the dominance of State by Religion is very much alive today in the young State of Israel; and the liberal or Reform and Conservative Jews and their rabbis are subject to what amounts to mediaeval discrimination at the hands of the Orthodox who, having organized politically, exercise their power to limit the liberties of those whose interpretation of Judaism differs from theirs. In Israel today, although I am a regularly ordained rabbi, I could not perform a wedding ceremony.

The issue is contemporary and pertinent all through Latin America, where the Church has profoundly influenced internal and external policy. Anti-clericalism is strong. Furthermore, the influence of religion in politics is a frequent source of irritation. In countries where Roman Catholics are in the majority, the rule of equal rights for all is not infrequently disregarded on the grounds of "public order." It is not only interesting but important to note that in those countries where a Religion enters politics as a bloc to achieve sectarian goals, irritation is rife and anti-clericalism is strong. The American tradition declares that true freedom does not mean one law for a man in one place and another law for the same man when he happens to live in another place.

There is some reason to fear the rise of anti-clericalism in this country because of sectarian intrusions into areas of sovereignty rightly assigned to the state. Take the issue of public funds for education under sectarian auspices.

In the *St. Louis University Law Journal*, the Rev. R.J. Henle, S.J., writing on the legal aspect of state aid to religious schools, presents an interesting plea for state aid to religious schools. He says, "One of the main intentions in the Public School System of America is to make free education available to all citizens. Any citizen may avail himself of public help in educating his children by sending them to a public school. Unfortunately, however, this excellent intention and purpose is implemented in an unrealistic manner. The very form which the aid takes in the concrete sets up a religious qualification or rather disqualification. For the simple fact of the matter is that many religious persons cannot send their children to the public school without violating their conscience. . . .

"We cannot, as Americans, simply say that this religious scruple is their own affair; that they may come to the public schools if they want aid, but, if they choose not to do so, that's their own affair. This religious conscience is one of the factors in the case and must be taken into account by the government. Religious liberty and the prohibition of religious qualifications are meaningless unless they relate to the precise pecularities of each type of conscience."

Father Henle is right when he insists that "the religious conscience is one of the factors." He is wrong in suggesting that the government does not take it into account because it does not subsidize Catholic parochial schools. The government, indeed, recognizes the religious factor when it does *not* insist that all children in the United States must go to public schools; it recognizes the religious factor when it offers the citizen the option to send or not to send his children to public schools. And this is as far as the government can reasonably go if state and church are to remain separate.

The question of state subsidies to Catholic schools has aroused partisan feeling in France for many years. The renowned Roman Catholic, François Mauriac, was questioned by Catholics in the recent controversy on the subject. His reply is an example which proponents of the idea in this country may well regard. Mauriac said, "You do not have the right to make a vote which engages the destiny of France and the peace of a world depend on a controversy around the school. . . . The important thing is not that our ministers go to Mass, but that they restore the State and serve justice obediently. . . . Search for the Kingdom of God in its justice; where there is justice there is the Kingdom of God."

No one will question the right of any group to support its own system of education. The public school system is a peculiarly American institution. It is also the one broad area where the children of America can learn to live together in mutual respect and sympathy; where the child is not Protestant, Catholic, or Jewish, or white or colored, but an American. Any and every effort to secure public funds for the support of schools under sectarian auspices is a threat to the American public school system and should be resisted.

The recent attacks on Dr. Conant, which were not limited to his position as a leading educational authority but aimed at his appointment as High Commissioner to Germany, were vicious, not so much because he pointed out the divisive nature of our "dual systems of education" (that is, the public and parochial schools— after all, not much more than ten per cent of the school population attend private or denominational schools), but rather because he declared that enemies of the public schools "should be smoked out." Many devout Roman Catholics believe that parochial schools should continue to be supported entirely by the Catholic people. We do not need nor want more sectarianism in our public schools, but more religion in our churches and synagogues. The question of welfare and health services, school lunches, and transportation are complex issues still to be resolved. In general, no one would want to deprive any child of the benefits of such a program provided the basic principle of separation is preserved.

All Religions have from time to time come into legal controversy with the civil authority. Trouble begins when the claims of any Religion flow over into areas of conduct affecting all citizens. Many irritations and pressures result from the overlapping and often conflicting claims of church and state sovereignties.

Intrusion of the Religions into the area of politics invariably means the secularization of religion rather than the religionizing of the secular. I do not refer to those broad issues of social justice and human welfare where the Religions must speak fearlessly, rallying public sentiment to do justly, to work righteousness and to walk humbly with God. I refer to the intrusions of the organized Religions, as Religions, and for sectarian ends. Such intrusions make for tyranny as history eloquently testifies. For the tyranny of the Religions can be just as ruthless as the tyranny of Fascism, Nazism, or Communism. It is moved by the same monopolistic presumptions and exercises the same autocratic power to suppress difference and force conformity. It bans free communication with the outside world and rings down an iron curtain. It is therefore necessary to watch carefully any tendency of any Religion to claim sovereignty in areas that the state claims as its own.

The matter of censorship is likewise a subject of heated controversy, involving the principle of whether any denominational group has the right to impose its own point of view as to what people shall see or not see, hear or not hear, read or not read, upon all the citizens of the nation. It is not straining a point to urge that we look behind the surface of things in this matter of censorship, to ask whether there is a pattern of control behind all these attempts to eliminate books from curricula and library shelves; to exclude Planned Parenthood organizations from Welfare Boards and doctors associated with them from hospitals; and to prevent physicians in public hospitals from giving birth control information to non-Catholic women. Jews, Catholics, and Protestants who support such undemocratic procedures imitate Communist practice. Perhaps the only solution of all these problems which are caused by conflicting claims to sovereignty, lies in the voluntary adjustment of all Religious groups to the broad tradition of separation. If however, there be those who refuse to accept separation except as an expedient and not on principle, and who continue to exert pressure for preference or privilege, then it may be necessary, as has been suggested, to secure separation by further clarifying amendments to the Constitution. Indeed, several joint resolutions looking to this end have already been introduced in Congress.

Difficulties also arise from the policy of some Religions to insist on what Anson Phelps Stokes calls "voluntary isolation"—that is, the prevention of free association between the groups in order to preserve the integrity of the group. Jews, Protestants and Catholics have all been guilty in this regard. While the determination to protect the integrity of the group is understandable, the value of free association in a democracy should not be minimized.

Roman Catholics should never forget that, despite persecution by the ignorant and biased, intelligent and liberal Protestants rose again and again to their defense. It was a Protestant lawyer and a Protestant judge who protected the sanctity of the Confessional. Jews should never forget the support which Catholics and Protestants have given in securing and maintaining for them the integrity of their rights and status as citizens. And Protestants should never forget that Catholic and Jewish judges and justices have been keen to protect and quick to defend the traditional separation of church and state. Nor should they ever take advantage of their majority status. Men in public life everywhere, but particularly in Washington, could reveal much about the silent pressures of all the Religions and other groups. If they voice their real opinions, they might jeopardize their political futures. Faced with this dilemma, they avoid issues or straddle them. But the people are fed up with smoke screens and double talk. Our country and its people have always appreciated and rewarded moral courage. Evil thrives in darkness. He mistakes the temper of the nation who hesitates to speak the simple truths. Pressure of particular groups, whether directed to some foreign goal or to some advantage to themselves within the nation, are intolerable today within our democracy. Publicity and moral courage are the best weapons against them.

To put it in its larger perspective, as I see the problem, it is this: Two ideas are engaged in combat for the conquest of the world. The East-West controversy is but one sector of a far-flung battle line. The church-state controversy is but another sector in this Titanic struggle to conquer the minds and spirits of men—nothing more nor less.

The real issue is this: Shall the human mind be free? Shall the spirit of man, endowed with an insatiable curiosity, with an invincible desire to tear aside the veils, to extend the horizons of apprehension, be cramped and limited, or shall it be given freedom to enlarge and transform itself? Totalitarianism and authoritarianism are the same, whether exercised in politics, economics, or religion. They constrain and shackle the mind. The old-world mind is mature, sophisticated, profound, but it is often weary and disillusioned. It seeks refuge in an irrational romantic mysticism or in an abandonment of independence and an uncritical acceptance of authority. Disillusionment and sophistication have often led it to the cold, calculating realism of Machiavelli or to casuistic, arbitrary and even inquisitorial methods from which the truth-seeking, straightforward, independent mind recoils as from something less than honest or kind.

Such minds assert they are humanitarians, yet one feels a cruelty born of an aloof pride, an inflexible sense of superiority, and a will to dominate. They assert they are realistic, but it is the realism of a system of logic that does not really concern itself with human beings or compassion. They and their kind might remake the world, but it would be an authoritarian world. In the past men with such minds have killed a man to save his soul or have turned him over to the secular arm for punishment, because punishment is not their prerogative! They have done these things, have logically justified them, and have felt a sense of satisfaction that they had promoted the will of God!

The mediaeval mind can teach us profundity and appreciation of the complexity of life, and it holds up the dream of unity under authority. Our American dream is of that harmony which must be won through voluntary association for ends that are larger than parochial, particularistic, nationalistic, or sectarian.

Where church and synagogue seek to censor, control, distort, or pervert the simple convictions dominant in American tradition, and to which the vast majority of Americans of all creeds yield unreserved loyalty, they cease to be the voice of religion and pass over into politics.

Finally, the creeds and denominations, in demanding freedom for themselves, have two obligations: the obligation not to abuse that freedom by attempts to secure special privileges, treatment, or status for themselves; and the obligation to desist from and to relinquish any demand that is inconsistent with those universals which underpin all the religions.

We have a long way to go. And basically what I am talking about is an attitude of humility. Such an attitude will mellow our controversies, chasten and refine our own particular faith and may help check the demands of the over-zealous.

All who love our American democracy and all who care to work for its future must work and pray and live together in this spirit.

* * *

The revolt against reason, the excessive emphasis on authority and the intrusions on the sovereignty of the state that are evident in much Christian thinking and practice, are manifest in Jewish thinking and practice. Among Jews the revolt against reason takes on a number of forms: a reversion to ceremonialism for its own sake, the presumptions of an arrogant and renascent orthodoxy, and the mystique of Jewish nationalism as the norm by which a Jew's loyalty to Judaism is measured.

There are those who propose a return to ceremonies and formalism. Liberal Judaism is criticized for being colorless and negative, and among Liberal Jews one finds a sort of reversion to conservative forms, particularly in the public worship of the synagogue and in a renewed emphasis upon ceremonial observance. It may be true that Liberal Judaism lost much of the poetry and color of our faith in its endeavor to re-interpret our tradition in terms of modern life. But the spirit of Liberal Judaism has been challenged by this reversion and its universal insights have been relegated consciously or unconsciously in many quarters to second place. This is a period, however, of transition, and the genius of Judaism as well as the genius of America will in time bring about a better balance between the particularistic in Judaism and the universal ideals which are its *raison d'être*.

But official Orthodox Judaism insists on the observance of religious ceremonials that are all too frequently ignored by orthodox Jews or observed by them perfunctorily as the last thin thread of sentiment that binds them to things that once lifted their hearts. I believe in ceremony as the poetic expression of religious truth, as an eloquent means of interpreting religious ideals, and as a discipline for conduct. Ceremonial observance, furthermore, when rooted in tradition and kept fluid and vital, makes for survival, but ceremonial observance alone in Orthodoxy or Reform is hardly the authority that will revitalize the religious life of the American Jew, that will give it ethical consciousness and power, and flow over into nobler political and economic relations.

Jewish Orthodoxy in America, moored to traditional anchors, regards both Liberal and Conservative Judaism as a threat to the integrity of the faith and aggressively attacks them. The Beth Din, an organization of Orthodox rabbis, vigorously condemned one Reform congregation that accepted certain classic principles of the liberal faith as a condition of membership: "They have deliberately, wilfully, and defiantly departed from the inner fold of Israel through their open spurning of the roots of our Torah and brazen denial of God's commandments and promise concerning the dietary laws and Eretz Israel. . . . They have thereby deserted the true faith and have placed themselves beyond the Pale and outside the fold of Israel. . . ."

In the Reform Movement itself there is a considerable controversy not only on the question of re-instituting ceremonial and traditional practice, but on the question of the relation of the Jews of the world to the State of Israel. Beholding the weakened religious convictions generally characterstic of our times, many rabbis and laymen turn to the dynamic of Jewish nationalism as an instrument of survival. They believe that the State of Israel is the symbol of world Jewish unity and that Jew and Judaism will survive only as the Jews of the world unite to support Israel. Jewish political nationalism is offered as a surrogate for the older authority of Jewish life which lay in the disciplines of a religious tradition.

The Jew was not always as concerned with himself as he is today, except in reference to the observance of his faith. In the darkest periods of his history, when forced into ghettos, when expelled from his home or when burned at the stake, the oppression visited upon him did not cause concern for survival. This did not enter his mind. What did consume him was that he be true to his faith and faithful to his God. Today the emphasis is on survival. The major considerations of Jews are motivated by fear of extinction.

In the last half century, a startling change has taken place in the thinking, feeling and even conduct of American Jews. The consciousness of brotherhood, a normal thing in an historic people, has been transformed into a consciousness of nationhood and nationality, secular in its foundation and political in its action. Anyone familiar with Jewish history could have predicted this phenomenon, for Jew and Judaism of any given period, have always been influenced by the events and spirit of that period. Today, an accented nationalism, while characteristic of a general world malaise, is characteristic of Jews and Judaism.

In Jewish life and thinking, particularism on the one hand and universalism on the other, have been persistent elements. One or the other was dominant according to the conditions under which Jews lived. All Jewish and Christian scholars agree on this point from George Foote Moore to Leo Baeck, Salo Baron and Mordecai Kaplan. In times of peril, ranks closed and the particularistic was dominant; in happier times, the universal was dominant.

I suggest, however, that the feeling of Jewish unity is something quite different from modern Jewish political nationalism; it is now as it always was, the conscious kinship of a people whose religious tradition enjoined them to "be a blessing" and serve the world.

Jewish nationalism has injected hysteria and hate into Jewish community life, stunted its normal growth and poisoned its wholesome atmosphere. It has employed a vocabulary of sonorous phrases—"totality of Jewish life," "walk with dignity," "self-hating Jews," "minimal Jews," "hush-hush Jews." One yields to the suspicion that the nationalists are victims of the inferiority complex they are so prone to ascribe to those who oppose them.

But Jewish nationalism, even though it has achieved greatly in

Palestine, represents a retreat from the authority of Judaism to the authority of Jewish peoplehood. Indeed, in some of its manifestations it is a cynical rejection of obvious ethical and moral standards.

One can only hope that the controversies in the Jewish communities of the world, centering around Israel, will be mitigated; that the passionate nationalisms of the Middle East might be brought to reconciliation as responsible nations unite not only to restrain the Arab and Israeli extremists and prevent war, but as they assist the Arab countries and Israel to set their economies on a stable basis, develop their resources and elevate living standards, so that they will learn to work together as free and democratic nations in a free and democratic world.

Thus the task of Jew, Muslim and Christian today would seem to be, not an emphasis on the group, the personal, the particularistic, but rather on the universal.

However, no such spirit animates Reform and Liberal Judaism in the United States today. Official Reform Judaism and its leadership have retreated before the authoritarian claims of Jewish nationalism. Changes have taken place but they are not in the genius of Reform. The Union Prayer Book was revised. But how? By the introduction of more Hebrew! Often ceremonies are re-introduced, not re-interpreted, as if the mere return of the form will revive the spirit. Services are longer, as if more time meant more religiosity. Loyalty to the God of our Fathers is often subsidiary to loyalty to the Jewish people. Concern for the soil of Palestine competes with concern for the soul of Judaism. Not infrequently, official Reform has been faithless to its own spirit. Reform has welcomed into its congregations erstwhile members of Orthodox and Conservative congregations who had little knowledge of Liberal Judaism and less patience with it. These new members have changed the face of Reform. Reform has grown in numbers, but it is in danger of losing its integrity. It has been swept from its moorings by the tide of nationalism.

Reversion to the authority of Jewish nationalism may be understandable and explainable in the setting of contemporary Jewish history, but it is sad and it is wrong. And unless Reform and Liberal Jews reject these reversions to an authoritarianism of peoplehood or land, there will be no Liberal or Reform Judaism in the United States in another quarter century. For the children of Reform congregations will reject the melange of nationalism, particularism and ceremonialism, combined with a weak and uncertain universalism, which contemporary Reform offers them.

Remove from our synagogues the acid fruits of expediency! Train a generation that will be indignant at injustice, sensitive to suffering, dedicated to usefulness and humbled by a vivid sense of responsibility to God. Liberal Judaism in America could take on new life because it would then be true to its own spirit. It would not break with the past nor ignore the realities of the present. It would move into the future with the confident strength of those whose roots go deep but whose branches reach toward the skies.

The Jew can make his characteristic contribution to our American life out of the universal insights of Judaism. The Jew should seek and will find his authority in his Judaism. He can put the warmth of reality into the abstract principles of justice, decency and compassion; he can do his utmost to transform the pious phrase "human brotherhood" into a passion for fellowship; he can contribute out of the genius of Judaism to the agonized efforts to prevent world catastrophe and build an enduring peace.

It may well be that in the game of international politics there are no more cards to play, particularly in the Middle East, and that resolution of the dilemmas and problems, the fears and suspicions and hatreds of that troubled region can be achieved only if the humanitarian and universal religious emphases of Judaism, Mohammedanism and Christianity are brought by Jewish, Muslim and Christian leadership into the unhappy picture.

* * *

The Catholics say, "Back to the authority of the Church." The Protestants say, "Back to the authority of the Bible," and, of course, their interpretation of the Bible. The Jews say, "Back to the authority of the people and the land." Thus in the Religions as well as in politics, the cry is "Back . . . Back to authority . . ." But is there no other authority? An authority which summons man to face ahead, an authority which recognizes the dignity of man, which does not do violence to his intelligence nor exploit his cherished sentiments for smaller goals? It is the authority of man's unfulfilled potentialities, the authority of freedom as yet unrealized, the authority of his inner search for dignity and worth, the authority of the human spirit, linked with the divine spirit and longing to break its shackles, to take wings and soar!

* * *

This is no time for liberal Christians and Jews to fear the future, to revolt against reason, to return to irrational mysticisms or systems which elevate blood or breed or creed to places of dominance. This is no time to revert to authoritarianisms which the experience of the race has rejected. I am convinced that one of the things we need most at this time is just a little more downright common sense. God's existence is not at stake. Man's freedom is. In liberal religion, reason is not the destroyer; it is the great corrective and its exercise releases the flow of God's revelation.

We cannot—nor would we—blot out the past. But we must learn what to remember and what to forget. We have learned that there is a community of interest among the authoritarians in politics and economics which can be met only by a community of interest among the democracies. Let liberal religionists, too, learn that their freedom and their future depend upon recognizing their own community of interest, as they face the forces in revolt against the authority of reason.

Where shall we find the authority we seek and on which the intelligent may with confidence rely? Is there any such authority? There is!

It is the authority of the free human spirit in an autonomous moral order, an authority that has been won through sacrifice and the blood of martyrs. This authority of the liberated, self-disciplined mind has wrested from all the tyrants of the past new areas of achievement, has opened new and larger horizons, has broken many shackles and set slaves free. It has given man a sense of indignation at wrong, has fortified his will to make right that which is wrong, has deepened his sense of social obligation. It has glorified his instinct for compassion. In the past it has been expressed in political, economic and religious organizations, discarding some, and creating others. Today the authority of this disciplined yet liberated mind of man must be increasingly expressed in politics, economies, and in the Religions of today. No authority of individual or party, or group or nation or race, or even of the organized Religions, can supplant the authority of the free mind. It is autonomous. It does not derive from force ruthlessly used or from ignorance wilfully imposed. It derives from the living spirit of life itself—from God!

We are witnessing today one of the great moral conflicts in man's age-old battle to beat down the brutal, the elemental, and the irrational, and to elevate reason in the life of man.

Before man can respect his fellow man and deal honestly with him, he needs to recognize his own endowments and respect them. Through the use of his reason he needs to re-examine his convictions constantly and to purify his faith. He needs to discipline his feelings and submit them to the control of reason. Because man had not yet learned this lesson, the world of business became a deadly, ruthless competition. The world of politics elevated shrewdness and cynicism and exalted power. But man needed something more than what the traditional Religions offered him. And so he created other gods to worship—the state, the soil, the nation, or the leader. Human relations became fraught with dishonesty and greed and selfishness; war and the threat of war, wreak their mighty vengeance on man's denial of the highest in him, that which relates him to his Maker—his reason.

This is a period of great danger for liberal religion. But it is a period of great opportunity for liberal religion and for the release of greater reason not only in religious thinking but in all human relations and institutions.

Each generation has to break the shackles of the past which bind it to the outworn and the useless. But its job is not done when that is done. It must learn to forge new shackles for itself. Each generation has to find its own authority within itself, in its sense of need, in its longing for justice and for human brotherhood. It has to seek and struggle for them in its own way. The weapons of the struggle change with time and the years. But the ideals are changeless principles on which to build, and goals towards which to work. They represent the deathless in man and that which links him to the Divine.

Man may revolt against reason and yield to the authoritarianisms of the past or the present, but the victory will be only temporary. Freedom may go under for a while. It rises again in the passion of men to claim its dominance of the human soul. The free spirit of man will create new institutions, interpret old laws in new spirit. Perhaps that is the way in which God works through man and uses him. Reason is one instrument of revelation.

As William Ellery Channing so well expressed it, "Once an idea has taken strong hold of my mind, it cleanses the soul in its divinity, its union with God. I call that mind free which does not copy the past nor live on old virtues, but forgets which is behind and rejoices to pour itself out in fresh exertion. I call that mind free which protects itself against the usurpation of society, which does not cower to human beings and feels itself accountable to a higher tribunal than man. I call that mind free which jealously guards its intellectual rights, calls no man master, contents itself with no idolatrous faith, receives new truths as an angel from heaven and, while consulting others, inquires still more of the oracle within itself. I call that mind free which sets no bounds to its love, recognizes in all human beings the image of God."

CHAPTER FIVE

Catholics, Protestants and Jews In America

I WANT Jews to understand their Christian neighbors better and Christians to understand Jews better. Even more than that, I want to see intelligent comprehension by Christians and Jews of each other's traditions and ideals, as well as sympathetic cooperation in those fields where they have much in common. I believe America needs this mutual understanding and cooperation and that the need is a vital one today, one that is at least as important as anything else. With these things in mind, I shall try to interpret the American Jew to his fellow Americans, and to show how the impact of contemporary events has affected the mind and heart of the Jew, particularly the Jew born here, one with roots deep in the American tradition; the tensions that tear his heart, the dilemmas he faces, the problems which confront him merely because he is a Jew; the hopes that stir him, the goals he seeks.

It is well for Americans to understand how a Jew rooted deep in both the American and Jewish traditions, loving both, yielding complete loyalty to both, looks out upon the contemporary scene. The vast majority of the five and a half million Jews here, though they have been not so long in residence, have achieved a striking synthesis of their Jewish traditions and their American ideals. It is a grievous injustice to divide Jews into a Western European group and an Eastern European group, to say that all good is embodied in the former and bad in the latter.

Most American Jews are sons or grandsons of immigrant Jews from Poland or Russia, no matter if they speak broken English, English with a Yiddish overtone, or English with a Harvard or Brooklyn accent; and have won through to complete acceptance of the American ideal, which they treasure as they do their very lives. In a sense life hurls many of the same challenges to us all. But for the Jew, because he is a Jew, the challenge is sharper, the tensions more tightly drawn. Furthermore, the American Jew, just because he is a Jew, finds himself in certain areas of conflict which his Christian fellow citizens do not experience because these border lands of feeling are unfamiliar territory to members of the majority group, because they are the majority. The Jew ordinarily finds it difficult to talk about these conflicts; perhaps he would rather not refer to them. It is for this reason that Jews are often silent and that Christians find in the eyes of some Jews a strange mystery as of distances and worlds that separate them.

The problem is not only one of anti-Semitism, though that is part of it. The Jew has been but one of the many scapegoats in world history. But wherever a minority group was subject to discrimination, the security of the majority was weakened. The disenfranchisement and segregation of the Negro does not make life in our southern states more stable or wholesome for the white man. No nation is secure where people are divided against themselves, where groups are self-conscious, jealous of their privileges, where leaders seek to preserve their personal power, where thinking is provincial, and where classes are arrayed against each other.

So far as Jews are concerned, it matters very little in the long run what happens to a few thousand or a hundred thousand of them. With us prejudice and persecution are familiar experiences; we are a people well acquainted with sorrow. But it does matter a great deal what happens to America. It matters to us and to our children. It matters to the world. None of us can ride out of the present national problems on the back of anyone else; we shall all lose in the end.

The task of responsible leadership in America today is to lay before our citizens the larger loyalty to America which embraces the lesser loyalties of group and class, the larger loyalty without which the lesser loyalties cannot be saved, nor even the greatest loyalty of all, the loyalty of man to his Maker. It must envision the American that might be, and, in a world which flouts democracy and invades and destroys the sanctities which are the inherent privilege of every human being, resolve to realize in ever greater measure, the America of our hopes and of our dreams.

The scapegoat technique, whether the scapegoat be Jew, Negro, Puerto Rican, Catholic, or a member of any other group, has no place in our country. We need a new dynamic in American life. Something that will set us on our feet again; something that will override the selfish interests that tear the nation asunder; something so great and compelling that it will sweep us up by its lift, so that we may see beyond the lesser loyalties of personal, group or class interest, give us a vision of what we might be as a people and the strength to realize that vision. We need a new dynamic in our America. It must be, it can only be, a dynamic of the spirit; a dynamic that will once more make men proud to work and to give work; that will overcome the unwholesome lethargy which has infested the nation like a plague and sapped its very vitality, the willing eagerness to take from the public trough, to let someone else pay for your ride, and to let George do the worrying; a dynamic so strong it will make mighty men and mightier interests yield to its compelling power, sweeping greed and ambition and coldness from their hearts; that will make employers deal decently with their workers and pay an honest wage for an honest day's work, that will make the workers scorn to shirk their tasks and make them turn their backs upon unscrupulous leaders, that will bind the masses and the classes into one brotherhood, sharers of the American spirit; that will sweep prejudices away and mold us into one people; that will make the city but an extension of the home and the entire nation one household, one family. We need some such dynamic in America, one not built on hate or blood or soil, nor on the backs of any victims among her citizens, nor at the sacrifice of essential liberties and the freedom which is the heritage of all men. We need loyalty to that greater America we might build, a loyalty larger than the lesser loyalties, harmonizing, embracing, transcending them all.

Whence shall come the dynamic for this larger loyalty? We have tried force, and we have failed in that. We have tried law, and we have failed in that, too. From the ancient shrines of church and synagogue might well come the moving impulses, the dynamic that will spiritualize the nation and set the faces of our people forward and their feet on the march, to build for our sons and daughters a nation dedicated to freedom and justice and peace, the true democracy.

One might contend that the hard irreducible facts of organized Religion stand in the way of the realization of this dream; that institutions and their traditions, leaders and their ambitions, and the nature of man himself stand in its way. True, we shall never move an inch forward unless we face frankly the hindrances, limitations and obstacles within Jewish, Catholic and Protestant groups which prevent complete cooperation. These difficulties arise out of the faith and practice as well as the psychology of Christian and Jew, and it is good to list the most important of them.

Obstacles imposed by Jews and Judaism:

1. Many Jews, because they were among the last arrivals in America, bear the scars of their European experience. Old World fears, suspicions and inhibitions and present conditions here and abroad that strengthen them, disturb Christian-Jewish relations.
2. The divisions among Jews make united thought and action well nigh impossible.

3. The Jewish will to maintain the integrity of the group often prevents free association and easy collaboration between themselves and non-Jews.
4. The influence of Jewish nationalism among Jews has intensified Jewish consciousness of difference and set it up as an end to be served in itself.
5. There is widespread ignorance among Jews of the liberal Christian position or indifference to it.
6. The need for defense against anti-Semitism consumes a great part of the Jew's time and energy.

Obstacles imposed by Protestants and Protestantism:
1. Past and present Protestant experience has built up fears and suspicions of Catholics and Jews.
2. Millions of Protestants are still keenly aware of Protestant denominational distinctions which claim their first attention.
3. The dogmatic assumptions of some Protestant groups is resented by Catholics and Jews.
4. Protestant groups frequently boycott Catholics and Jews in the spheres of business, politics and social relations.
5. Catholics and Jews remember Protestant vendettas against them, exemplified in the past by the APA and the KKK, and more recently in many Protestant circles, by a quiet, unorganized, insidious but effective discrimination.
6. Catholics and Jews object to Protestant endeavors to write into the laws of the nation what to others is a matter of personal privilege, but what to many Protestants are religious principles: prohibition, for example, or Blue Law legislation.

Obstacles imposed by Catholics and Catholicism:
1. The large immigrant Catholic population has brought here old world antipathies and inhibitions.
2. Historic Catholic suspicions of Protestants and Jews and prejudice against them are still present in interfaith relations.

3. Catholics want to preserve the integrity of their church and their faith by introducing the European practice of state taxes for parochial schools.
4. The Catholic assumption of complete and authoritative truth and traditional Catholic practices often make cooperation difficult.
5. Catholics frequently boycott Jews and Protestants in business and politics.
6. The Catholic attitude toward church and state and the claim of the Catholic church to authority over certain areas in which, according to the American tradition of separation of church and state, the state is acknowledged supreme, is rejected by Protestants and Jews.

All these difficulties are real but given time and forbearance, education and the American spirit will reduce many of them as points of irritation. There is, however, a difference between the Protestant and Jewish points of view, on the one hand, and the Catholic viewpoint on the other, which, with all the goodwill in the world, cuts through to something so fundamental, that it must be understood and accepted before any cooperative program between the religious groups can be successful. It arises out of Roman Catholic doctrine itself, particularly out of the claim the church makes for itself and its followers, one that is inherent in the Roman Catholic position, the authoritarian attitude of the church. There can be no argument about this claim or against it, for it is essentially the Roman Catholic position. Without it there would be no Roman Catholicism. Being what it is and claiming certain things for itself, the church has to maintain this philosophy and promote its program in accordance with it. We must not only understand these claims, but accept them as facts in American life, if we hope to achieve any adequate appraisal of the situation. But having done this, it becomes necessary, with equal frankness, to point out the effects such Roman Catholic claims have upon the relations of Catholics with their fellow citizens of other faiths and of no faith, and the influences which this Roman Catholic attitude sets moving in American life.

Hilaire Belloc, a devoted Roman Catholic, in his book, *The Contrast*, refers to "the necessary conflict between the civil state and the Catholic Church, where the two are not identified." He goes on to state in a very revealing and frank chapter, "The Catholic Church is in its root principle at issue with the civic definition both of freedom and authority. For the purpose of the state, religion is either a universally admitted system or a matter of individual choice. But by its definition, one which is the very soul of Catholicism, religion must be for the Catholic, first, a supreme authority superior to any claims of the state; second, a corporate thing and not an individual thing; third, a thing dependent upon authority and not a personal mood; fourth, a guarantee of individual freedom in all that is not faith. Now it is clear that between the attitude here defined and the attitude of the non-Catholic state which proposes tolerance—that is, the definition of religion as an individual concern—there is a conflict. For tolerance means indifference to those acts and doctrines which the state treats as private, coupled with enforcement of certain acts and doctrines which the state insists upon treating as universal."

The issue is nowhere more clearly stated. Coming as it does from a Roman Catholic of unquestioned loyalty and never having been denied in official Catholic quarters, it must evoke a similar frankness on the part of all non-Catholic Americans.

There cannot be two authorities in the same area. When a state says, "This is my prerogative," and the church says, "No, it is mine," the issue is joined.

The most obvious example is in the realm of education. Believing as it does, the church sets up its own educational system, the parochial school paralleling the public school supported by the state which has come to be the American way. Most of us, while we regret that the church feels it necessary to conduct its own school system, abide by our democratic tradition and take the position that if Roman Catholics wish to set up their own school system and pay for it, they are entitled to do so. We may not agree with them. We may even deplore the sharpened sense of difference which such schools unquestionably engender, but we feel the Catholic has an inherent right as an American to give his child the sort of education the demands of his faith declare to be necessary. We admire the Catholic for his determination even at a personal sacrifice to fulfill the obligations of his Religion as they are taught to him. So far, so good.

But when attempts are made, as in Louisiana, in Ohio, in some western and other states, to secure funds from the public budget to support the parochial school system, the American citizen senses a danger. He believes that the public school has come to be the American educational way and that it is a good way. Every man has the right to educate his children privately as he so desires, but he must bear the burden of that education or send his children to the state supported schools. He must not expect the state to support a school system maintained for the promotion of any particular religious faith. The non-Catholic American sees in this attempt from some Roman Catholic quarters, a threat against the public school system. Once the principle of state support for religious or denominational schools is established, it could mean the final breakdown of the American school system. The non-Catholic American sees in the public school system one of the finest instruments for the promotion and maintenance of democracy. Any such union of church and state is reaction and not progress. It makes no difference that the American public school is the outgrowth of denominational educational efforts. The average citizen means to maintain the American tradition of public education and resents Catholic efforts to obtain public funds for the support of parochial schools.

Catholics argue that they are taking a burden from the state by educating millions of their children. They explain the parochial schools at present are pinched financially. They declare that for them to discontinue their system and transfer the expense of maintaining it to the state would entail an even greater public tax burden. This argument meets with no hospitable response. Non-Catholic Americans will defend and protect the right of their Catholic fellow citizens to maintain their parochial schools, but the public schools are here to be used, and they are the heritage of all our American children. Those who do not want to use them must be willing to pay for any system they insist upon substituting for them.

But it is not only the demand for a share of the educational budget that is a point of irritation among non-Catholics, it is the philosophy which exacts this demand.

Take for example the Catholic position on birth control. The Roman church has a definite point of view. Because it is the point of view of the church, it is held to be authoritative truth in the realm of public morals. There are only approximately thirty million Roman Catholics in the United States, and in disagreement with them is the state which may not enact sectarian legislation and the general public which does not accept the Catholic position. Most physicians and citizens in general want to have birth control information made available where it seems to be socially necessary. The Roman church says, "No"; other Americans say, "Yes"; and the church, believing as it does, cannot do otherwise than oppose. The majority of American citizens can do no more than press for a change in the law. But the spectacle of the church as a church attempting to incorporate its particular beliefs into the law of the land, and to impose its position upon the nation, creates a grave source of irritation against Roman Catholicism. Non-Catholics take the position that if the church desires to enforce such procedure among Catholics, they can understand, for that is a matter between Catholics and their church. But for the Roman church to attempt to write its doctrines into American law and attempt to force non-Catholics to abide by church doctrines amounts to a union of church and state and a violation of the American democratic way. The issue was recently fought out in New York City when an attempt was made by the church to prevent the dissemination of birth control information upon advice of physicians in areas where it would be socially beneficent. The attempt failed, but much ill feeling was engendered. Similar situations prevail in Massachusetts, Connecticut and other states today.

The question is not only how far is the church justified in pressing its claims to enforce its denominational practice upon American citizens, but also how far will it go, believing as it does in its own authority.

To make the picture complete, the same objection must be voiced with reference to the increasing number of attempts by some Jews to operate Jewish parochial schools, or by Protestants, to promote Protestant parochial schools. No group has the right to inject into the law of the land its peculiar religious or denominational predilections. The same thing applies to pressures for Sunday Blue Law legislation by Protestants, and against Sunday legislation by Jews. But these instances among Protestants and Jews are not general authoritative attitudes of these groups, they are sporadic attempts made here and there which are more or less successful, depending upon the willingness of local politicians to yield principle to pressure for votes.

Irritations between Catholics and non-Catholics in America rise out of some Catholic attitudes in international politics. The church, for instance, was unquestionably persecuted in Mexico some years ago, and there was deep feeling in certain Catholic quarters that the American non-Catholic population was not sufficiently indignant or sympathetic. This apparent lack of indignation and sympathy rose out of the non-Catholic's belief at the time that the difficulties of the church in Mexico came about through the church's insistence upon authority in certain areas which the State of Mexico claimed as its own. There were other factors in the situation also, economic and political as well as religious.

We Americans have an instinctive distaste for any union of church and state; it arises out of the very fundamental principles of the republic. There is no sympathy among us for religious persecution; we abhor it. But the general feeling among liberal-minded people is that the modern state must free itself from the century-old domination of the church in areas over which the state claims sovereignty.

A similar instance was provided in the attitude of the Catholic church in the United States toward the Franco revolt some years ago. Many elements entered into the Spanish civil war. Unquestionably one was the opposition of the church to the republic and its natural resentment against any regime which would lessen its power, its privileges and prerogatives. Despite the fact that the population of Spain was overwhelmingly Catholic on both sides, the majority of American Catholic officials, dignitaries, and leaders took the insurgent side. Attempts were made here by some American Catholics to prevent meetings in sympathy with the government. The Loyalists were called Reds. Non-Catholic citizens who favored the government were attacked as radicals. Of course there were persecutions of Catholics in Spain, especially in the first days of the rebel uprising; and there was truth in the Catholic charge of Communist influence in the Spanish government. On the other hand, the church as a church was anti-Government and pro-Franco.

The Catholic church has officially taken the position that it is not interested in securing any preferential rights or privileged positions for Catholics in America. The long record of Catholic contributions to the life of America and the integrity of character of those who speak in its name are recognized and appreciated. However, there are factors in the situation which cause Protestants and Jews considerable apprehension, and concerning which it is just as well to be utterly frank.

Are Protestants and Jews in America to understand that the church makes a distinction between those places where it is in the majority and those places where it is in the minority? Would it not be well for Catholics earnestly to consider the natural inferences which Jews and Protestants may draw from this condition; namely, that were it ever to come to pass that there should be a Catholic majority in the United States, the Catholic church—as evidenced in Italy or Austria and Poland—would be given a preferred position and its members political privilege to the detriment of non-Catholics?

In the light of a papal encyclical of some years ago wherein the doctrine is set forth that where Catholics are in the minority the majority must tolerate them, because Roman Catholicism is truth, but where Catholics are in the majority it is incumbent upon them to assume the responsibility to have that truth dominate, Protestants and Jews might well have cause for apprehension.

It is perfectly obvious that an organization world-wide in its scope, with precedents and traditions to guide it which are centuries old and believed to be infallible, with its adherents living under varying conditions and in all lands, with memories of temporal power, should of necessity deal with different situations in different ways. The program of the Vatican and its point of view, to be consistent, must meet each situation as its needs demand, bearing in mind always the philosophy and authority of the church. And that is just what Protestants and Jews fear: the practical and inevitable program of the church authoritarian philosophy. Neither the official documents of the church in our times nor the records of history dissipate that fear.

In his volume *Catholicism and Christianity*, Cecil John Cadous states:

"In 1885 in the encyclical *Immortale Dei*, Leo XIII blamed all states that granted 'equal rights to every creed so that public order may not be disturbed by any particular form of religious belief.' In 1887 the *Defensa Catholica* declared that 'true charity consists in opposing one's neighbor, injuring him in his material interests, in insulting him and in taking his life, always supposing that it is done for the love of God.' In 1888 Leo XIII issued another encyclical, *Libertas Protestantissima*, in which he laid it down that the State ought not to tolerate all Religions alike, but ought to profess only that which is true, viz.: Catholicism; that liberty of worship is the degradation of liberty and the submission of the soul to sin, that 'the more a State is driven to tolerate evil, the further it is from perfection.' The Church, he said, 'does not forbid public authority to tolerate what is at variance with truth and justice, for the sake of avoiding some greater evil'; nevertheless 'although in the extraordinary conditions of these times, the Church usually acquiesces in certain modern liberties, not because she prefers them in themselves, but because she judges it expedient to permit them, she would in happier times exercise her own liberty . . .' In the same document Leo condemned the view of those who, as regards the Church, 'maintain that it does not belong to her to legislate, to judge or to punish but only to exhort, to advise and to rule her subjects in accordance with their own consent and will. By such opinion they pervert the nature of this divine society, and attenuate and narrow its authority, its office of teacher, and its whole authority.'

"Seeing, however, that heretics were guilty of rebelling against the lawful authority of the Church, were a danger to the spiritual safety of others and were a general menace to the social order, it follows that the proceedings taken against them did not constitute persecution—for persecution is unlawful and unjust, and 'the Catholic Church forbids the least injustice to anyone.' Nor are the victims rightly regarded as martyrs; for they suffered, not on behalf of Christian truth, but on behalf of their own mistaken opinions. Nor was the treatment they received cruel; it was indeed painful but so is all chastisement. Even burning alive is not necessarily cruel punishment; for it gives the sufferer ample opportunity of penitence before death.

"If now the Church as a perfect society has a right to coerce heretics and apostates by means of temporal penalties, if toleration on principle is indefensible because it presupposes religious indifference, if the treatment which the Church formerly meted out to heretics was neither cruelty nor persecution but the just chastisement of real guilt, it surely follows that—opportunity given—the Church will coerce heretics in the same way again.

The accuracy of this very simple inference is strongly confirmed by the repeated declaration of modern Catholic authors that the reason why the Church today has given up persecution is the regrettable fact that circumstances—in particular political circumstances—have changed, that States and governments no longer profess the Catholic faith, and that no State today is willing, as in the middle ages, to lend its power to the execution of ecclesiastical penalties . . . There have not been wanting responsible Catholics who have had the frankness to state explicitly the inevitable conclusion . . . In 1901 Father Harvey said in reply to a question put to him about Protestants during a mission in New Jersey: 'I do not doubt if they were strong enough that the Catholic people would hinder, even by death if necessary, the spread of such errors among the people and I say, rightly so.' "

The logic of the position is, of course, inevitable.

In the Catholic Encyclopedia, 1912, Volume 14, page 7696 this sentence occurs, "The final conversion of the old religious state into the modern constitutional State, the lamentable disaffection of the majority of states from the Catholic faith, the irrevocable secularization of the idea of the State and the coexistence of the most varied religious beliefs in every land, have imposed a principle of state tolerance in freedom of belief upon rulers and parliaments as a dire necessity."

That means from the Roman Catholic point of view that granting religious freedom is only a matter of "dire necessity" brought about unfortunately by changed conditions. For Protestants and Jews the granting of religious freedom is not a dire necessity nor the end result of the compulsion of circumstance. It is a matter of principle, voluntarily accepted as an obligation due in the same measure to one who differs from us as to ourselves. This is apparently the unbridgeable chasm between the position of the Roman Catholic and the position of the non-Catholic.

For Roman Catholics toleration and equal rights for all the

Religions are hedged about with an amazing structure of casuistry. For Protestants and Jews it is a simple and inalienable human right.

The whole mesh of fine-spun logic in the Catholic position is made necessary by the axioms of the church in its relation to human life and events, by her claim to complete possession of truth in thinking and practice and the obligation upon her to maintain and spread that truth. Grant the premises and the rest logically follows. But that is just what the liberal mind may not, cannot, grant; and there is where the fundamental conflict enters. The Roman Church lays claim to authority in certain areas. She cannot do otherwise on the basis of her primary assumptions. But the liberated mind as well as the modern state say, "No, this is my domain." Difficulties naturally follow.

The church is thoroughly consistent but her very consistency makes her position difficult. Jews and Protestants may worship together; Catholics may not join in public worship with Jews and Protestants. Although this rule is on rare occasions not followed, it represents a logical attitude deriving from the church's assumption not only that she is the legatee of the faith that redeems, but also that she possesses the means of redemption. "Rabbi Lazaron," said a priest to me, "it is not that we have no beliefs which we hold in common. We have. But the things that we share are not so important. The things on which we divide are most important. For we share together only our belief in God."

Nothing could be clearer. The church cannot afford to give her followers the impression, which common or community worship would naturally give, that Roman Catholicism is just one of the Religions.

What to do? No arguments by non-Catholics will avail. Religion is so intimate and personal a matter that every man must decide these things for himself without the intrusion of well-meaning but perhaps misguided outsiders. Protestants and Jews and non-Catholic Americans must accept the situation as they find it and make the most of it, cooperating where they can with Roman

Catholics, and certainly not permitting whatever convictions they may have about the rightness or wrongness of the Catholic position to interfere in their personal, business, professional, and social relations with them. To be civilized is to know how to live with others who differ from you. No Roman Catholic should be held at a disadvantage or discriminated against merely because of his faith.

I believe American Roman Catholics are loyal American citizens. Like the followers of other faiths a vast majority are simple, honest folk, for whom the church is a source of comfort and strength. Should it come to a choice, I believe they would say to Rome, "In matters spiritual, we follow you; but not in those things which affect our American citizenship." However, the implications of Catholic doctrine are obvious and it cannot be by chance only that difficulties have arisen in those countries where the population is preponderantly Roman Catholic and where the priesthood intrudes into matters political.

On the other hand, Roman Catholics must understand that non-Catholic Americans will not permit them to fulfill the logical implications of their theology within the United States or in the relations of the United States with other nations. They must be prepared for the fact that non-Catholic Americans will oppose, by the democratic processes of the ballot, any attempt to write Catholic dogma into American law, American education or American life. Freedom was won at too high a cost. The conflict lies there, and it may be that with the years it will become more acute. Let us make every effort to keep it restrained and civilized.

The lines of friendly communication between Catholic and non-Catholic Americans must be kept open. Jews and Protestants must understand and appreciate the demands the church makes upon its adherents. And Catholics must try to understand the reaction their position sets in motion among us. With goodwill on both sides, if the church recognizes the fact that it is only one of many (no matter what it may feel about the truth of its position) and exercises the moderation and cooperation which must be at the heart of a healthy democracy, there is no reason why Hilaire

Belloc's prediction of possible violent conflicts here as in the old world need come to pass. Above all, there must be an increase in understanding and cooperation between Catholics and non-Catholics in all areas where the general welfare is at stake.

Roman Catholicism has something to contribute to American life. Its constant insistence on the necessity of faith, man's dependence on God, the inscrutable mystery of the world; its disciplines which refine and spiritualize, its submission of all things to the final test of religiosity—these are challenges which are needed in our national life today, and the Roman Church, with its singularly effective organization, can be a powerful instrument making for the spiritualization of American life.

The Protestant spirit of Luther is as important today as it was in his time. I remember how stirred I was as I stood by that great monument to the leaders of the Protestant Reformation in Geneva. I thought of Protestantism's fundamental emphasis upon the freedom of the individual conscience and man's right to reach out and find his Maker. I thought of Protestantism's brave contemporary challenges in dangerous areas of industry, politics, war and peace.

As a Jew I can appreciate and share in these great Catholic and Protestant emphases and in the expression of them, for both are basic in Judaism. But Jews must not be drawn as Jews into the Catholic-Protestant controversy. We should not align ourselves as pro-Protestant or pro-Catholic. However, it must be recognized that the spirit of Judaism is more akin to the liberal tendencies in American Protestantism and may feel more at home in that company. Jews must keep the American ideal in mind and cooperate with all who labor to defend and promote it.

* * *

For the purpose of clarification rather than condemnation we have been discussing the obstacles to cooperation. Happily there are many possibilities as well. For Jews, Catholics and Protestants there are two areas in which we may and should work together:

we may and should insist upon spiritual values as the basis of human life; and we may and should insist that those values be expressed in economics and politics and in human relations.

I do not mean to interpret the spiritualization of American life in creedal or denominational terms. I would rather see a Jew who has thrown off the disciplines of Judaism find religion through Christianity than that he have no religion at all. Scores of Christian student religious leaders on the campuses of the country are guiding Jewish youth to an understanding and appreciation of the truths and beauty of Judaism. This is startling and gratifying. And Jewish student workers on campus often do the same for Christian students as opportunity presents itself.

I remember a lad at one of our well-known colleges in the East. Something he said at dinner at the fraternity house made me realize he was troubled. "I've lost so much of what I brought here from home and I haven't found anything to take its place. I still pray, though not with the same feeling of conviction." He was not a mollycoddle. He was a normal, wholesome lad of twenty, manager of one of the athletic teams and very well-liked by his fellow students. For nearly three hours we talked alone that night. He told me the story of his background and training. He had come from a Christian home and had all that that implies, but he was worried and wandering. At the end he gripped my hand, and, looking me straight in the eye, he said what many other Christians had told me before though none had put it in such a simple, dramatic way: "I've been waiting for over two years for this talk. I never would have believed it if someone had told me it would be a rabbi who would lead me back to Jesus!"

This sort of thing can be done all along the line. Perhaps some Christian with soul aflame for the living God can light a fire in the hearts of Jews who may be cold to words which come from the lips of a Jewish teacher. Perhaps he can bring home the reality of God as an intimate experience where I cannot, and turn Jewish footsteps back to the synagogue and the faith of the fathers. The important thing is that that be done. No man to whom God's reality has ever been a living experience can ever be the same again.

Jews and Catholics and Protestants can unite in a common effort to express these values of the religious life in the fields of industry and politics, not as individual Jews and Catholics and Protestants, not to the glory of church and synagogue, but to the general welfare of all the people at a critical time. This is already being done through cooperation between the Central Conference of American Rabbis, the National Catholic Welfare Council and the National Council of Churches of Christ in America. The social justice programs of the three groups make interesting reading as they reveal a common social idealism and social goals.

There are practical ways in which the religious communities may cooperate. Some years ago the Maryland Legislature was called into special session to enact a relief bill. The relief situation was appalling. It had become the football of city and state politicians, each "passing the buck," dodging responsibility and blaming it on the other. Twenty-eight days of the session had passed in constant wrangling, with no relief legislation enacted. It appeared that disagreements among the various factions would cause the Legislature to adjourn and the thousands of relief cases would be handled—well, somehow! The late Catholic Archbishop Michael J. Curley, the Protestant Episcopal Bishop Edward T. Helfenstein and I sent a public telegram to the Legislature in which we said:

"The spectacle which now presents itself raises our indignation. The cheap political trickery, the sinister trading, the evil pressure of selfish groups and persons, the arrogance of special interests, reveal a situation which is shameful and intolerable. . . .

"We would remind Senators and Legislators that they were sent to the state capital by the vote of the people. . . .

"We solemnly call upon the State Senate and Legislature . . . to enact the measures for relief. . . . A civilized community can do no less. In the name of God and our common humanity, we demand that this thing be done."

The evening papers played up the situation. The Legislature resented and writhed. But a relief bill *was* passed.

I shall not forget the message Archbishop Curley sent me after reading the wire he was asked to sign: "It's pretty strong, but I'll go with you!"

A more recent striking example of Catholic-Protestant co-operation is occurring in Massachusetts where the Roman and Protestant churches have united to carry on a campaign of education against gambling, crime and corruption.

What do I mean by the dynamic of religion and the common task of church and synagogue to spiritualize American life?

One day I was tramping through a forest of hemlocks in western North Carolina. My companions were a lumberman, a geologist, a painter, and a poet. Giant trees rose ninety feet without a limb until their spreading branches at the top shadowed the trail in a cool and quiet peace. The lumberman looked at the trees, commented upon their size, estimated so many feet of lumber at so much per foot and exclaimed: "What a treasure is here!" The geologist pointed to the rock formation, at the waving lines in a cliff across the glen where the story of some cataclysm centuries ago revealed itself, and spoke of the possible mineral resources that lay beneath our feet. The painter watched the play of light and shadow along our path, the drifting clouds, the pastel blue which hung from the sky upon the distant ranges like some magic curtain. He wanted to catch this glorious beauty on a bit of canvas. The poet bade us cease our talk and listen to the forest sounds. I listened to them all. Each one had spoken from the angle of his particular interest.

My mind worked another way. I saw the lumberman's prospective wealth. I thrilled to the geologist's dramatic story of creation. The beauty to which the painter directed his eyes evoked a response in my heart and I yielded to the spell of the poet's word and thought. Then I asked: But what is the golden thread which binds them all? What is the mysterious power that makes them one? I see beyond this wealth of lumber, the hidden power in some tiny seedling years ago which now stands monarch of the forest. I am silent in wonder as I think back through the ages and behold the miracle of unfolding creation, or when I contemplate man's capacity to sense beauty and imprison it in form or color; man's power to think, to dream, to hope, to struggle; man's capacity for friendship or love or sacrifice. What golden threads bind all these together? The idea of the one God! The grandeur of the natural order, man's pursuit of truth, his appreciation of beauty, his drive toward justice and holiness—it is all one. Where the lumberman sees lumber, potential wealth, I see God. Where the geologist reads the rock-writ story of the ages and sees earth's natural resources, I see God. Where the painter sees the possibility of a lovely canvas, I see God. Where the poet interprets beauty in terms of philosophy, I see God. One God, one Mind, one Will, one Beauty, one Love.

We are all human beings. We have not only bad tendencies but good tendencies. We are capable not only of selfishness and greed but of good will and love. We were created that way. We are all of us caught up in this mysterious experience called life. We are parts of a process which, though at times it seems objective, cruel, ruthless—at other times seems intimate, personal, kindly. For every catastrophe I can point to a blessing. The thunderstorm that wrought havoc to crop and habitation cleanses the air, waters the ground, and evokes the ministrations of healing and helpfulness for the stricken and forlorn. For every disease a frantic effort is made to discover cause and ultimate cure. For every famine there are outstretched hands to feed the hungry. In your own personal life you have known heartache and frustration and despair; but you have known also work and struggle and achievement, the tenderness of friendship and love, the joy of fulfillment. You do not comprehend it all but faint intimations come to you, whispers that tell you it is "all a part of one stupendous whole"; that you, one single being, are significant in the scheme of things. Some intelligence is attempting a glorious adventure with nature and humanity as materials. You are necessary not only to an adequate explanation of the story of life but necessary also to its happy conclusion.

Will you work with that mind and will and love we call God? He expects it of you. Will you yield to the promptings of the true, the beautiful and the good within you and so in your own life further this mystic process of evolving glory in which we all have a share?

The late Dr. Frankwood Williams put it: "Man's fear drives him to seek security where he will never find it—outside himself in defensive-offensive group alliances with laws, rules, regulations and eventually armies, and to sanctify in the name of group law and order the very things he has been fleeing from. . . . Our bondage is to ourselves . . . an individual's freedom comes first from within, secondly from without. . . ."

But I ask: What is the force from within that must be roused to action and brought to dominate man's life? It is the mysterious ingredient which defies the microscope. It is the spirit of man. Also it is man's instinctive acknowledgment of what is right, his capacity for friendship, his consciousness of brotherhood. These are constructive forces just as potent as destructive forces in the creation of a finer social order. Any analysis of the principles that must motivate social betterment which ignores them, ignores at least the half of reality. And this half is the sphere of religion. The force within has been built up laboriously through the centuries, through the discipline of experience, the ministrations of religion which always have held up to man a picture of what he might be if he would. Even beyond all this centuries-old training in religion, there is the instinctive impulse of man to relate himself to the universe; man came to feel that life is worth-while, goodness is real, sacrifice is necessary, all things have meaning because he related himself to the eternal spirit. It was just this conscious relation to God that validated all his experiences. This was the dynamic that moved man.

When I say God I do not mean an old man with a flowing

beard riding on a cloud; I do not mean the Setebos of Caliban. I mean that mind and might, that will and love, that beauty and glory we sense in the world around us and to which in our best moments we feel related in an intimate and personal way.

I try to do the decent, generous, social thing because when I do some change takes place within me. I feel enlargement and exaltation. But I want to do it most of all because my horizons are widened, because I am conscious then of a friendliness in the universe, of an intimacy with seas and stars as well as with my fellowmen; because my life somehow seems caught up in the larger process of which I feel myself a worthy and necessary part; because my spirit for the moment seems to share in the cosmic process; because, in short, I then joyously recognize my kinship with God and my responsibility to myself and my fellow men.

Of course, I admit these things are not matters of scientific truth. There is no proof of God save that which rises out of the inmost being of a man. I know that not to all is given that poignant sense of His presence. I know, too, that religious institutions that have spoken in His name have in reality all too often crucified His spirit.

However, it is out of such sentiments, of which the institutions of religion are custodians, that the great social dynamic is born in the masses of men. Without this dynamic to restrain and humanize it, the social evolution becomes the social revolution; blood flows, pride of conviction runs riot as in the past, in the baneful institutions of Inquisition, pyre and pogrom, and in the present crucifixion of freedom in Russian Soviet dominated lands. Without this dynamic man builds on sand. With it man can build enduringly! Man becomes integrated in his universe. He will not feel that he struggles alone. He will not close his eyes to the evil in himself but he will seek to subdue it; he will not ignore it, he will sublimate it, because he believes in a power within and without himself that makes for righteousness.

We have never tried religion in this largest sense. In the spirit of man is the force that can be tapped to the everlasting blessing of society; the frank acceptance of the ultimate fact that within our-selves are areas of spiritual power which we have not touched, related to that source of inexhaustible power outside us which is God. Man needs to bring this overwhelming force to dominance in his life. Religion is the key which releases it. Once released it will go down into the depths of his being; it will lift him by its transcendent power; it will make vivid for him the noble poten-tialities he possesses. It will give him strength to realize them.

We are not only "a product of our civilization." We are the builders of the civilization that is to be.

This should be the contribution of the great Religions to Ameri-can life. This is the field for common work by Protestants, Catholics and Jews. This could be the new dynamic which could revive and lift the nation. Professor Robert Andrews Millikan (Nobel Prize in Physics 1923) writes:* "Essential religion is one of the world's supremest needs, and I believe one of the greatest contributions that the United States ever can, or ever will, make to world progress—greater by far than any contribution which we ever have made, or can make, to the science of government—will con-sist in furnishing an example to the world of how the religious life of a nation can evolve intelligently, inspiringly, reverently, completely divorced from all unreason, all superstition, and all unwholesome emotionalism."

What has religion to say to those who are caught up in the exhausting speed and pressures of life today? Has it any word of healing for those who are bruised, or consolation for those who weep in some great frustration or sorrow? Services of worship, rituals and creeds and sermons, all the visual and audible para-phernalia of organized religion often seem far removed from the hard facts of life, unrelated to man and his needs.

What are our own needs? We demand constant change, diver-sion, amusement, excitement. We need ever new, different and stronger stimulants. Our restlessness gives us no peace. Our times are not mature. "The World is too much with us."

* *Living Philosophies*, 1931, p. 53.

The choice is not between asceticism and hedonism. Religion says: Stop a moment, sit and think, dream and ponder . . . Let the mad procession go by . . . Send thought and feeling into the shadowlands and by some strange power that lies at the heart of life, the spirit comes back refreshed, the will renewed.

This "brave new world" will not be made only by those who *do*. It will be builded first in the minds of those who dream and plan. Trial and error are all right for the scientist's laboratory; but experimentation which involves the loves and hunger and lives of millions of men and women is a different matter. If men and women would stop moving for a while and do a little more thinking, perhaps we would be further along the road to that new world.

The restlessness, the apparent inability to keep the mind on one thing for any extended period, the hop-skip-and-jump thinking, the telescoped news, the acceptance of the superficial, the avid search for amusement—these aspects of our life could unfit us to cope with our national and international problems. When we lose our sense of values, the threat to our freedom will be obscured.

What is important? What must we bear constantly in mind?

The issue before the American people today is clear. It is not political; not which party shall be in power. It is deeper even than the serious economic problems which face us, more far-reaching than the questions of government relation to labor and the unions, to business, finance, the great corporations, or the average citizen. The issue is the preservation of the American tradition of freedom and the democratic organization of society.

As I ponder the events of the post-war years, it seems to me that upheavals usually occur under two conditions: one—where a small group in power uses its power to oppress and the masses of the people have no recourse other than violent overthrow of tyranny. This usually results in the substitution of one tyranny for another, as in the case of Russia where instead of the dictatorship of the classes which obtained under the Czarist regime there is now dictatorship of the Communist party. That is not the American way. Or two: revolutions result where conflicting interests, groups, classes and parties in a nation have reached the point where they neutralize each other. Paralysis of political and economic progress follows and some sort of seizure of power by one of the groups breaks the deadlock, as occurred in Nazi Germany. Here, too, the method sought to remedy the evils destroyed liberty and brought oppression. That is not the American way.

Both these factors are working in the American scene. Politically, economically, lines are being drawn, groups are forming—each voicing more or less sincerely its own shibboleths and defending its own special interests. If the situation develops along these lines, undoubtedly there will be trouble ahead. Let both sides be warned. When you destroy the rights of the meanest citizen of our country, you lay the foundation for the destruction of your own rights. The men who underpinned the rising power of Mussolini and Hitler did not realize that their turn would come next—as it did. A dictatorship is like a cancer. It is impossible to limit the objects of its oppression to any class or group; it will go to any end to maintain itself in power.

Our task is to solve the national problems in an American way. Can't we forget our partisan interests and mass our best intelligence in one great national effort? Even the winner will lose if his group rises to power at the sacrifice of any other group. Just as no body is healthy one of whose organs is diseased, so no nation can endure with large groups discontented or denied opportunity. It is reasonable to hold that no political, social, or economic order is in itself sacrosanct. It endures so long as it makes for human happiness and progress. That is, I believe, the law of life.

What we today must learn is to see our times in the great perspective of history. I do not advocate any particular system or machinery. That must be the task of statesmen, economists and engineers. I do plead for an abandonment of the present heated partisanship on all sides—for a moratorium on group and class selfishness, an attempt to solve our problems in the American way so as to preserve the American tradition.

Certainly on the credit side this might be said: A force is rising among us which will not be denied. It gathers power each day. We must move forward to meet it. That force is the power of the social conscience, the mystic power—"not ourselves"—which makes for righteousness and justice as the foundation of enduring human relations. This idea has already come into industry, politics, education, criminology and philanthropy. It is a far cry from Gary to Willard and Swope. The social conscience is aroused. Politics concerns itself more and more with the social problems of the community and the state. Education emphasizes adjustment to the social organism and development of effectiveness and richness of life with one's fellows. Criminology condemns not only the criminal but hails the social body to the bar and indicts society for making the criminal what he is. Modern philanthropy seeks not only to relieve immediate distress but to create conditions which prevent it. This is the leaven that is working in American life, though there are influences seeking to destroy it. But if it is nurtured and fostered and suffered to guide and lead us, we shall witness such a conquest of the human spirit as has never been witnessed in history—the triumph of the American idea.

There are terrible lessons that we must learn from contemporary events. There are encroachments here and there upon the American ideal—violations of rights of free speech and public assembly. Deny any man the right to speak and you have weakened the principle which establishes your own right. There are exploitation and all manner of injustice among us. Attempts are made to becloud the issues. There are those who serve our country ill, though they drape the flag unctuously about them. There are those who would label every liberal idea "red" and who see a Communist behind every effort to better conditions. There are those who would crusade against Godless Communism, even to the extent of bathing the world in the blood and agony of nuclear war—and that in the name of religion.

No man who loves God will excuse the ruthless destruction of religious values and the Communist campaign of atheism. But let us look further for cause and reason. It is because religion lost contact with the longings and needs of the masses of the people, closed its eyes and ears to the cries of suffering and oppression, turned its back upon and refused to accept its divine function— it is because of these things that religion in Russia and in many other places has been persecuted. In the days that are to come God will try our hearts. Especially great will be the temptation to try to repress the rising will for social betterment. If the synagogue and the church become the handmaids of the state or defenders of the *status quo*, if we play the harlot to the god of things as they are, we are doomed!—and we deserve to die.

We cannot fight Godlessness with weapons of hate or force. Religious teachers have too often permitted themselves to become tools of evil, the bondservants of oppression and war. Monstrous things done in the name of patriotism have had—and in some quarters still have—the sanction of organized religion and men have therefore lost faith in religion and God because of those who speak in religion's name. The strength and power of religion lie in the unselfishness and goodness of the men and women who profess it. Religion cannot be strengthened by prestige nor underpinned by financial power. No one knows the place where Moses was buried, and Jesus died on a cross between two thieves. But the power of their spirit rolls down through the centuries transforming the lives of men. Glorious edifices and the drama of a magnificent liturgy do not enhance the power of church and synagogue when the spirit of God has fled! History shows with a strange eloquence that there are no hates like the hates engendered by religion. I come from a people well acquainted with the nature of crusades. You cannot conquer the world for the God of love by a jehad of hate. Let Christian and Jew beware of such tactics! They will divide our citizens against each other at the very time when we must preserve our national unity. Religious institutions in these trying days are not going to save themselves by defending the *status quo* under the shield of David or the cross of Jesus.

Let Christians and Jews in America beware of adopting any such measures under the camouflage of defending religion or under the banner of the living God.

There are some people who would have Christian and Jewish spokesmen bleat in pious terms about God and religion as if the twain were utterly separated from human conduct. We religionists believe that justice is real and loving-kindness more than a phrase. We believe these things rise right out of the very depths of life and that we ignore them or deny them to our peril. These things are because God is.

We cannot divorce religion and God from the abuses and wrongs of the day, from the sins and exploitations and misery of our times, from the fate of the unfortunate, the oppressed and the disinherited. If we do, then all reality has fled from the shrines of church and synagogue.

The task of church and synagogue, as I see it today, is to throw its passionate faith in human brotherhood into the balance; to resolve to make that faith live in human relations; to interpret it in the removal of every vestige of economic serfdom and in the recognition of the partnership of labor and capital in a democratized socially sensitive and just industrial order.

If church and synagogue join any crusade against liberalism, men will turn their backs upon them. They will destroy themselves. They can preserve themselves and help preserve our democratic institutions if church and synagogue set their hands to the task of righting the wrongs that afflict our society today. They must have patience with each other. Wrongs built up over the years cannot be righted in a day. There must be forbearance and a heightened sense of justice, a deepened sense of compassion rooted in a revived and profound sense of our responsibility to God. There must be a feeling of humiliation and shame that our nation permits such wrongs as are visited upon the Negro. Church and synagogue may well intone the words of the Great Confession: *Ovinu malkenu chatonu lefonecho*—"Our Father our King, we have sinned before Thee . . ."

There is a passion for social justice among organized religionists as well as among the unaffiliated. It can be realized without the oppression and destruction of accepted values so characteristic of Communist methods. The difference between the Communist program for social justice and the religionist approach to social justice is that we refuse to burn down the house and all that is in it.

And the only lasting peace in industry, finance and international relations is the peace of righteousness. We in church and synagogue *must be true* to the solemn task we have assumed—to speak the great "thou shalt" and "thou shalt not" in the name of the Supreme Being we serve. We reject Fascism and Communism. We choose to work for a chastened, purified democratic political and economic order exemplifying the principles of God's fatherhood and man's brotherhood in human relations.

I believe a new spirit is in our land, a deeper feeling on the part of our citizens that none of us can prosper at the expense of the others, that human rights cannot be ruthlessly trampled upon, that people should not live out their years in poverty and undernourishment, that our vast material wealth and our intellectual and physical energies must be devoted to the service of all. Beneath all our extravagances, our superficialities, beneath even our lowered standards and political corruption, I believe a great tide is moving in the hearts of millions of Americans. Perhaps we've gotten a new glimpse of what we may make of our America. Indeed, the vision of the founders is revealed to us once more and in terms of our own day. In the providence of God we could set out upon the last stretch of the road, approaching that journey's end toward which the sons of man have falteringly struggled through the years. We could here in our America, under God, lay firm and sure the foundations of a society in which all men shall be free in fact as in name.

Here is our world with its hungry to be fed, its naked to be clothed, its maimed and sick to be given shelter. Here is the world with its orphans and widows, its nameless children and helpless outcasts. Here is the world with its vast combinations of capital capable of so much good and benevolence yet often used for selfish ends or for oppression and tyranny. Here is the world with its criminals and its prisons. Here is the world with its corruption in politics and the social order, with its religious prejudices, with its international hatreds. Here is the world with all its injustice and unrighteousness. What has man done to God's world?

Will we abandon this bustling, humming, buzzing orb of ours? Shall we retire into our shell and throw up our hands in holy horror, exclaiming upon what a wicked world this is? Shall we go into the sanctuary and sing sweet hymns and utter pious phrases? And shall we then expect prejudice to cease, expect injustice and corruption to be wiped out and a better social order to be created of its own accord?

To all of us there comes the challenge to rebuild the social order. Our problem is not only a matter of wages, conditions of labor, hours of employment and the general problems of social welfare. We should feel a passionate resentment at the injustice that has been visited upon large groups of individuals, the poverty and misery that desecrate contemporary life. We must cry out against injustice and oppression and unrighteousness. We must cleanse the dirty places of the world, bind up the wounds of those who are bleeding. Wherever oppression and injustice lift their heads, there we shall raise our arms as instruments making for the right. Wherever there are prejudice and hate and wrong, wherever there is lack of sympathy, we must lift our voices in a plea for understanding.

Furthermore, we are in duty bound to subject the present industrial situation to the keenest, most critical analysis. We must ask: Is the present industrial order making for a lessening of poverty and suffering in the world? We must ask: While this order is creating material things, what is it doing to the hearts and minds and souls of men? Is the industrial order making for the brotherhood of man? If not, why? Is it because the present economic order considers itself outside the realm of ethics?

We must fearlessly declare that where the rights of property conflict with the welfare of humanity, property has no rights which need be regarded. We must declare that the economic and industrial order is not for the creation of buildings and profits only but for the creation of that opportunity for self-expression and for labor which is at once the highest privilege and the most solemn obligation of the children of men. We stand for the principle that behind our obligation to ourselves and our fellow men and consecrating that obligation there stands the figure of the everlasting God. "Unless the Lord build the house, they labor in vain who build it."

Christians and Jews, before the challenge of our common tasks, let us be patient with each other, trusting each other, helping each other, as we work together for human liberty and justice and for ordered progress toward the realization of God's Kingdom on earth.

CHAPTER SIX

The Controversy Among Jews

Nationalism will not save the Jews here or in Israel.
Judaism will save the Jews in Israel and everywhere else.

FOR Jews the name Palestine touches profound depths of sentiment and, for religious reasons, this feeling is shared to a considerable degree by non-Jews as well. Vast sums have been contributed by American Jews to develop the land, and a million Jews have found haven and home in Israel. There is no difference of opinion among Jews on the question of helping maintain what has been built with so much energy, idealism and sacrifice.

I wish to make my position clear. I opposed the establishment of the State of Israel, but I believe its destruction would be one of the tragedies of history. This, too, I believe: that the powers most influential in creating Israel—the United States, Britain, France and the Soviet Union—are morally bound, as is the parent organization, the United Nations—to see to it that Israel shall survive and prosper so long as it observes those standards of policy and conduct which make for comity among the nations. Certainly those Jews who feel themselves members of a scattered nation, who constitute the State of Israel, are entitled to security.

My quarrel is with the philosophy of Jewish nationalism and its aggressive intrusions on the American scene. The Zionists never recognized the profound motivations of Arab nationalism. Even in 1921 on the occasion of my first visit to Palestine, then mandated to Britain, I found an active Arab nationalism, resentful of the Zionist attitude. Jew and Muslim had lived together for centuries in reasonably good relations. There was never the persecution of the Jew in Arab lands which characterized Jewish experience in Christian lands after the church triumphant succeeded to the power of the Roman Empire. If Jewish immigration to Palestine had been presented as a cooperative venture benefitting both peoples—for the Jews who wanted it, a national homeland, and for the Arabs an opportunity with the help of Jews to develop the resources of the land, lifting the standards of the Arab population— the present unhappy situation might never have arisen. The early Jewish settlers in Palestine lived in harmony with the native population. They were welcomed. It was only when Jewish nationalism as a philosophy, with aggressive Zionism as its program, came into the picture that matters went from bad to worse, with all the bitterness, bloodshed and tragedy of the last years as a consequence.

Meanwhile, I trust that Arab-Israeli and Muslim-Jewish problems which disturb the Middle East—the questions of the Arab refugees, the principle of repatriation, the definition and guarantee of borders and the internationalization of Jerusalem—will be settled in time with the help of the United Nations, so that the work of reconstruction can go on in the entire area, the living standards of all its people be raised, and some measure of stability be established. This will require compromise and concession on both sides.

This chapter concerns itself with Jewish nationalism, its philosophy, techniques and aims, what it has done and is doing to Jews and Judaism in the United States. Jewish nationalism in Israel is a natural attribute of statehood. Jewish nationalism in the United States is an unwelcome intruder.

The philosophy of Jewish nationalism may be summarized as

follows: The only place in the world where a man born a Jew can lead a normal Jewish life is in Israel. The Jew is different and feels his difference. The Gentile feels that the Jew is different. There is no cure for anti-Semitism; even in free and democratic nations the position of the Jew is unstable. What place he may have won is only temporary and subject to the whim of the majority. He may be deprived of his rights by any quick turn of the wheel of fate. The Jew must recognize this unhappy status and accept it, performing his duties loyally and devotedly as long as he can, but needing his nation, Israel, to which he may go in the day of wrath, which is bound to come; for the Gentile world will always misunderstand and persecute the Jew. Jews living outside Israel will ultimately disappear unless they are bound to the State of Israel by strong psychological and emotional ties. Jews must either emigrate to Israel, or if they do not, they must support Israel with their wealth, their know-how, their man-power and their political influence.

It should be noted that among American Zionists there are varying degrees of acceptance of the above propositions. Zionists themselves are divided. Some reject the idea that all Jews must live in Israel to achieve a complete Jewish life; many reject the proposition that soon or late they will be forced out of their present homes and have to live there. For instance, Mrs. Miriam K. Freund, President of Hadassah, the American Women's Zionist organization, in her opening address at the national convention of Hadassah, October, 1958, said, "While Hadassah believes that Aliyah (immigration to Israel) is important to the Zionist movement, we do not agree with those who assert that Zionist ideology means that those who call themselves Zionists must give up the land of their birth and settle in Israel." Others oppose the idea that Jews outside Israel must organize in political support of Israel.

The propositions stated above, however, represent the basic philosophy of current Jewish nationalism and determine its programs and methods. It was alien to the Jewish mind until recent times.

Jewish nationalists assert, erroneously I believe, that Jewish nationalism is as old as the Bible. I myself once accepted that idea during the days when I was a member of the Zionist organization. One is justified in harboring the suspicion that the ancient prophets would hardly recognize contemporary Jewish nationalists as their comrades. Indeed, nationalists are the very type of ancient secularists and materialists whom the Biblical prophets denounced as false and blind leaders of the people. Contemporary Jewish nationalism rose out of the persecution and despair among the Jews of eastern and southeastern Europe. It was a reaction to anti-Semitism. The nations in that part of Europe were organized on the basis of racial and religious groups, each group enjoying civil and political, religious, and national *group* rights. The Jew fought for recognition as a national group in order to enjoy these rights. Jewish nationalism was never manifested except in places where these conditions obtained.

As Dr. Hans Kohn points out in his brilliant essay in the winter (1958) issue of *Menorah Journal,* "Zion and the Jewish National Idea," Theodore Herzl made anti-Semitism the foundation of his movement, as well as its compelling force. He actually considered anti-Semitic governments the best allies of Zionism and openly negotiated with the most anti-Semitic government of the time, Czarist Russia, for the advancement of Zionism. He points out that this obsession with anti-Semitism is the basic proposition of Zionism today: that the Zionist movement still operates on the theory that the worse the conditions are for the Jews in the Diaspora, the better it is for Zionism. While Zionists regard anti-Semitism as an unqualified evil, they also see it as a whip to be used to drive Jews to Israel. Last summer, at a meeting of the World Jewish Congress in Geneva (a Zionist organization), Dr. Nahum Goldman, the President, warned that "a current decline of overt anti-Semitism might constitute a new danger to Jewish survival."

Certainly the largest number of American Jews are not Jewish nationalists or Zionists. They are not members of the Zionist Organization of America, and they have no intention to leave here and go to live in Israel. They labored for the establishment of Israel because, conditioned by nationalist propaganda, they believed there was no other haven for their brother Jews, victims of oppression. They feel a responsibility for the State of Israel. Their motives are brotherly and praiseworthy and natural, but they seem unable or unwilling to recognize that there is a difference between philanthropy for Jews in Israel and Zionist and Israeli politics; nor do they seem to realize that their failure to make this distinction blinds them to the ugly facts of Jewish nationalism.

The Jewish nationalist seems to believe that for the millions who must live outside Israel the only future is to be annihilated in a process of assimilation. The Jewish nationalist agrees that the test of democracy is the attitude of the peoples to the Jews who live among them; but he apparently holds out little hope that this attitude can be civilized. He sees Jews outside Israel as living always in uncertainty or under recurrent threat of expulsion.

This view is a counsel of despair. It denies that there can be any progress or that freedom and democracy will spread among men. There have been and there will be crises in world history, ones in which suffering encompasses wide areas and involves many peoples —war, revolution, economic disasters. And the suffering of Jews is also recurrent. It parallels world disturbances or it follows them. Yet it occurs on its own and in periods where there is no great upheaval, though it is most frequently associated with some internal situation in the lands where it is found. The persistence and prevalence of anti-Semitism often distinguish it and give some semblance of truth to the claim that the situation is hopeless.

With the rise of the temporal power of the church, economic and political persecutions were added to religious persecutions. Generation after generation was conditioned by the idea that the Jew had rejected the true faith. He was a being apart. Special conditions of life had to be created for him. Laws and regulations were set up to govern his relations with his Gentile neighbors. He was forced to live in ghettos, to wear certain garments; his occupations were limited. Thus temporal and spiritual authority combined to set in motion a dual process of emotional and intellectual inbreeding which worked harm for the Christian and disaster for the Jew. The more the Jew was persecuted the more convinced he became of the truth of his Torah, his Teaching. He fed his pride from the same source. The world shut him out; but he had his God and God's gift, his Teaching.

It was an extraordinary but natural example of compensation. But like all compensations under such conditions, it did not make for completely wholesome attitudes in the Jew either toward himself or toward the world. Yet despite his unhappy experience of isolation, the Jew developed a culture of mind and heart. The list of our unsung saints is as long as the list of our martyrs.

Eighteen centuries of enforced isolation created much of what are commonly and wrongly called Jewish characteristics. Often the Jew is blamed for the very things which separation from the peoples had caused. The robe of shame which at times he was forced to wear later became to the Jew himself the badge of his tribe. The Gentile saw the Jew and said, "The Jew is different." And the Jew felt that he was different; and for compensation he accepted and glorified this difference in thinking and practice.

It was not until comparatively modern times that brave spirits arose who were not hindered by theological or other prejudices. A new wind was blowing over the world. The spirit of man was groping out of darkness toward the light. The longing for freedom stirred the hearts of the peoples. Leaders arose in many lands who entered the lists in the struggle for political and civil rights for all men; and Jews in those lands where freedom was realized shared the new-won blessing.

But the influence of the centuries was strong. The Jew struggling out of his sense of apartness after the first flush of freedom wherever he enjoyed it, was still a victim of the sense of a difference between him and his fellow men, a difference other than religious. The adjustment of the emancipated Jew was not complete either within himself or in his relations with his Gentile neighbors.

Furthermore, millions of his brethren still lived in lands where the old patterns were strong, persisting in the economic, social, political as well as religious status of the Jew. The Jew was constantly pulled back to the community suffering of his fellow Jews. The world considered him different. It did not treat the Jew as an individual human being who may be good, bad or indifferent, but it generalized on the old patterns and applied the general antipathy to the particular individual Jew. Good Jews, bad Jews, they were all alike, an alien clan to be persecuted or pitied, converted or tolerated.

The heart of the problem is, can anything be done by Jew and Gentile to break down the centuries-old misunderstanding? Need the Jew be always different, alien, foreign in Gentile eyes, or feel himself so in his own eyes? It is my belief that much can be done by both Jew and Gentile if they care enough about it; but neither can effect the change alone. Many Jews are inclined to throw up their hands and say, "Useless! Prejudice against the Jews is a fact in the world that can't be changed. Accept it; and also accept the Jewish consciousness of folk and national difference and proceed from there."

If one accepts these basic assumptions, there is logic in the position of the nationalists. Other people have a nationalist basis for their life. Among other peoples there are the religious, the nonreligious, the irreligious; so with Jews. Other peoples have a land of their own; Jews should have a land of their own. It is possible to see the rationale of this position and the activities that flow from it, *if limited to the State of Israel*. It is impossible for Jews outside Israel to espouse it and act upon it. Outside Israel Jews are a religio-cultural community, scattered like other religio-cultural communities throughout the world. But the Nationalists in Israel and here are not satisfied to confine Jewish Nationalism within the borders of Israel. They insist that their philosophy and program be applied here.

American Jews must choose between these two positions; and it is perhaps the most important decision which the Jew in America and the world has had to face for centuries. We cannot accept the folkist basis of Jewish life, and at the same time insist that we are followers of a universal religion. Jews here in the United States are either a scattered nation bound by ties of inescapable loyalty to Israel, or we are a religio-cultural community.

I do not accept the nationalist assertion that the Jew is unable to live a normal life outside Israel. The Jewish centers which produced the greatest contribution to our literature, other than the Bible, were outside Palestine. Nor do I believe that anti-Semitism is an incurable disease despite what happened in Germany under Hitler and the Nazis. Their brutal, incredible and unforgivable millionfold mass murders should never be forgotten, but should be remembered as one of the blackest pages of history. It should be remembered, however, that there were Germans, many of them, who did not agree with what the Nazis did and thousands risked their lives to feed, hide and protect Jews, half-Jews and quarter-Jews, targets for Nazi destruction. Germans who voiced their indignation were struck down; self-preservation prompted silence. I was there in 1935 before the worst of the holocaust. I saw; I know.

In this connection every American should earnestly ask himself, "What would I do if a wave of hysteria, hate and organized rioting threatened the security of any minority among us?" Every minister should ask himself the same question, "Where would I stand in the day of wrath? Would there be enough courage among us not only to protest but to oppose vigorously any such outbreak?" It is impossible to answer such questions, but it is worth-while to put them.

Anti-Semitism has become a burden on the Christian conscience. This is reflected in the recent utterances and conduct of Christian leaders. Let the Jewish Nationalists consult not the politicians whom they cajole or threaten, but rather the friendly and understanding non-Jews who are deeply concerned with the increase in anti-Jewish feeling brought about by some Zionists and Jewish Nationalist activities.

It can be shown historically that for all the reversion to the brutal which the last war and the present uncertain peace indicated, the progress of man is evident. Certainly the status of Jews in England, France and the United States and even in pre-Hitler Germany indicates an advance over the Middle Ages. Galileo's famous phrase "eppur si muove," "nevertheless it moves," is just as true of human relations as it is of the earth. Temporary setbacks do not change the general forward direction. Jewish-Christian relations are changing today. They are much improved; and it seems they will be better in the long tomorrow. The present anti-Semitism in some quarters is matched by an increasing understanding of the Jew and Judaism and by sympathy and support of persecuted Jews in every country of the world. When, for instance, his country was occupied by the Nazis, King Christian of Denmark is reported to have declared, "The Germans want to put the yellow badge on the Jewish citizens of Denmark; I and my whole family will wear it as a sign of the highest distinction." Priests and Protestant ministers in France, Belgium and Holland were jailed, tortured, exiled and killed for defending and helping Jews; the late Pope Pius XII saved the lives of thousands of Jews by opening Vatican City to Jewish refugees; and the present Pope John used his influence to emigrate thousands of Jews from Nazi-dominated Balkan lands. Thousands of lowly Christian folk, revolted by the inhumanity of the Nazis, justified their Christian faith by acts of compassion for Jews. As the magnificent statement of the Danish Bishops put it, "Notwithstanding our separate religious beliefs, we will fight to preserve for our Jewish brothers and sisters the same freedoms we ourselves value more than life. It is evident that in this case we are obeying God rather than man."

All but the most prejudiced see today that anti-Semitism is an instrument used by designing men to destroy society. To be hopeless is to reject the concept of progress in human life. If the status of the Jew be a test of democracy, Christian-Jewish comradeship can build its foundations sure and strong.

It will not be easy to break down the old patterns, to educate the people to an appreciation rather than suspicion and fear of differences. This is the Gentile's problem: to change the Gentile attitude toward the Jew. But Jews can help. The same historic factors which have conditioned the attitude of some Gentiles toward the Jew, have molded the Jewish attitude to himself and to the world. This is the Jewish problem: to change some Jewish patterns towards Gentiles. Unless both Gentile and Jew yield to a process of re-education nothing either does will ever be ultimately effective.

While some progress has been made, earnest Christians and Gentiles will realize that much more needs to be done. It is not enough to mobilize church and religious agencies and to pass resolutions in meetings and conventions. Unfortunately, relations between Christians and Jews are for the most part on an economic basis only. Except for occasional communal projects, contacts between the two groups are all too frequently limited to business. The Gentile sells to or buys from the Jew; the Jew sells to or buys from the Gentile. It is inevitable under such conditions, when the tensions of hard times come, that the strain is felt on its only point of contact. Temper Christian-Jewish relationships with the warmth of friendly intercourse, mellow them with the waters of understanding; let Christian and Jew enlarge the areas where they can work together as citizens for the common good, and we shall have a firm and wholesome basis on which to build bridges.

Gentiles, Christians and Jews, white men, black men, brown men, yellow men, Americans all, have shared in the cruel hardships and dangers of war; have seen that bravery and sacrifice are not the monopoly of any creed or color. They are found in all creeds and colors. All of us must carry over into the tasks of peace the nobler impulses evoked by the camaraderie of war. But because Gentiles and Christians are in the vast majority—there are about five and a half million Jews among the nearly one hundred eighty million people in the United States—a grave responsibility rests upon them.

On their part, Jews cannot dismiss the natural drive for homogeneity within any national group; it is basic. We must take this into consideration in any thinking about the future of the Jew in America. The Jewish nationalist and the folkist Jew give little thought to this important subject. They usually content themselves with castigating the non-nationalist Jew or attempting to floor him with the accusation, "You believe in American nationalism but not in Jewish nationalism." They assume the two are parallel; they are not.

Israel Zangwill in his essay on nationalism differentiates between nations which have crystallized and those in the process of crystallization. He classifies the United States as a nation in the making, because of the great varieties of people and cultures which have come to its shores. This idea, however, does not imply the development of an American nationalism that will exclude differences. We desperately need in our country a chastened and changed attitude toward minorities; but minorities on their part must recognize the deep impulse in every nation toward homogeneity. It is a natural tendency in a maturing state. Sometimes the impulse takes the form of legislative compulsion. More often in democracies it is a more or less conscious movement toward some inner harmony resulting from the free interplay of social, economic, political, religious, racial and cultural forces and groups. Majorities and minorities unfold, evolve, draw from, interpenetrate each other, contribute to and change each other; and the spirit of America working on our racial, cultural and religious majorities and minorities has wrought mighty changes in everything it has touched.

The current concept of cultural pluralism recognizes the values of variety and represents a praiseworthy determination to accept differences. But the Jewish nationalists should not delude themselves. Cultural pluralism is only a lodging for the night, a transition philosophy in the unfolding of American life. It is a wholesome but temporary concept designed to tide us over a period of adjustment. It may endure for an indefinite period of time, but there is an inexorability in the laws of social evolution, a movement through diversity, toward unity.

For the Jew to whom loyalty to a religio-cultural tradition is the foundation of Jewish solidarity, the preservation of this tradition in the land of his habitation is his important object. For the Gentile loyalty to his great tradition must be preserved. But suppose Gentile adjustment is met by Jewish adjustment. History gives eloquent and ample testimony to this possibility. Jews and Gentiles are living together, working together, some of them even praying together. Who can predict what will result from this easy, natural interplay? Perhaps something greater and nobler than our present concepts of Christianity and Judaism which will inform and change both. This need not make for the extinction of either but for the exaltation of both, each after its own genius.

American Jews can confidently reject Jewish nationalism and a folkist basis for Jewish life, and at the same time believe in Judaism as a universal religion and the comradeship of world Jewry as a religious community.

Fifty years ago in the United States there were few Jewish nationalists. Their influence was small. Initial response to Jewish political nationalism ran all the way from indifference to active hostility. This was so in all branches of Judaism and among all kinds of Jews and was expressed in resolutions of rabbinical and congregational organizations. This attitude of indifference or antipathy continued until World War I and the issuance of the Balfour Declaration, November 2, 1917, when Jewish Nationalism came upon the stage as a pressure group in American Jewish life. It was an aggressive force in international affairs during the decade of the 1920's. The advent of the Nazis deepened the burden of Jewish despair. The apparent indifference of the nations to the plight of the victims of persecution was more than the Jewish masses could bear. They themselves would find homes for their brethren in Palestine in what the Zionists had been calling even then Eretz Israel, the Land of Israel. And once they made this resolve, all the conditions and circumstances seemed combined to favor it. America needed a power to bastion the oil reserves of the Middle East against possible Soviet aggression. While the Soviet leaders, foreseeing the instability and persisting irritations a Zionist state would bring about in the area to their advantage, joined the United States in supporting its creation. A world-wide Zionist organization exploited not only the desperate refugee Jews, but the sympathy and self-reproach of the world and demanded the creation of Israel.

Several examples indicate how far chauvinism can lead even a people "well acquainted with sorrow." In his new book, *Exodus*, Leon Uris used the *Exodus* affair of 1947 as a dramatic incident in his story. The British government had established an immigration quota for Palestine, then mandated to it by the League of Nations, because it felt it necessary to pacify the rising Arab resentment. In the mid-summer of that year nearly five thousand Jewish men and women including some three hundred children left France for Palestine hoping to evade the immigration quota. British ships intercepted the *Exodus* and returned it to the Port de Bouc. The ship was a floating oven. France offered a haven and even permanent homes in that hospitable land. Despite the crowding and the horrible conditions, they refused to leave the ship. The real reason for this, it is generally accepted, was because they had been conditioned to believe that anti-Semitism was inevitable and they would go nowhere but to the Jewish homeland.

Another example of the lengths to which Jewish Nationalist chauvinism went is indicated in the tragic story of the *Patria*. In 1940 this ship carrying two thousand Jews destined for Palestine in violation of the British immigration quota was intercepted by the British Navy and brought to Haifa. The *Jewish Newsletter* of November 3, 1958, carries the story in shocking detail. "In accordance with procedure the immigrants were supposed to be sent to a British camp off Cyprus where they would be kept until the immigration quota would entitle them to enter Palestine legally. The Hagana, the Zionist Army of the time, decided, however, to carry out a political demonstration against the British immigration policy which limited Jewish immigration to Palestine to fifteen hundred a month, and decided to blow up the *Patria* rather than let the immigrants be sent to Maurizius. The plan was actually carried out." William Zuckerman, Editor of the *Jewish Newsletter*, continues the story, quoting from an article by Dr. Herzel Rosenblum, Editor of the Zionist Tel Aviv Daily, *Yedios Achronos*. Dr. Rosenblum was a member of the Zionist Actions Committee, the highest Zionist body before the establishment of Israel; a sort of shadow cabinet for the Jewish settlement in Palestine. Mr. Zuckerman translates Dr. Rosenblum's story of the meeting at which the final plans for blowing up the *Patria* were discussed: "This was in 1940, shortly before the affair of the *Patria* . . . A session of the small Actions Committee, of which I was a member, met in Jerusalem. At the table opposite me, sat the commander of the *Patria* project, A. Golomb (who died since) . . . When my turn came to speak, I rose and told the meeting openly everything I thought about this act, namely that this was not a fight against England, but an irresponsible, aimless mass-murder of Jews who had been saved from the European catastrophe. I added that if any one of us believed . . . that we had to fight the British by committing *hari-kiri*, let him commit *hari-kiri* himself; for *hari-kiri* is suicide and not an act of murder. I stated plainly that this road was open to Mr. Golomb but that he couldn't sacrifice other Jews for his 'policy', without first asking them, and particularly the children among them—a crime against which I openly protested.

"At this point Mr. Golomb jumped up and attacked me with his fists. But the people next to him at the table held him back. I must add that Mr. Golomb's fists, which I will never forget, did not provoke me as much as the servility of all the committee members, none of whom supported me. When I left the meeting, everything was in an uproar. I could not control my feelings . . . I thought of the Russian terrorists who refused to throw a bomb at the Czar because he was, at the critical moment, in the company of a child or woman. . . . But we murdered with our bare hands our own children, their mothers, sisters and dear ones, and yet everything is in order. Rejoice our people."

A third and final incident indicative of the chauvinistic fanaticism of the Nationalists was first given public expression in Cincinnati in May, 1950, in an address which the distinguished attorney Morris L. Ernst delivered at the Sixth Annual National Conference of the American Council for Judaism: "Roosevelt had an idea that what we ought to do with the people pushed around in Europe was to get up what he called a World Budget and let all the free nations of the world agree as to how many people they would take in as immigrants irrespective of race, creed, color or political belief. The President told me that he was sure that he could get so many into Canada, so many into Australia, so many into each South American country—and then he said, 'You know, we in the United States will be the last to open our doors because we are going back on our historic position of political asylum.' This was before the labor unions had taken their shift on the Immigration Bill. This was before the manufacturers had gotten a little wisdom on the subject.

"I went over to England on Roosevelt's hunch that I should speak to the British, the officials, to see if they would agree to take in 100,000 or 200,000 of the people pushed around by the Nazis. It was Roosevelt's hunch that if we could get England for a hundred or two hundred thousand and pick up a couple hundred thousand elsewhere in the world, nation by nation, we could then educate the Congress of the United States to go back to our traditional position of asylum: a position that is not only good from the point of view of compassion but is essential for the enrichment of our own culture.

"I went to England and I sat with officials and came back one day to the White House and I said, 'We're at home plate. That little island of Great Britain'—and mind you, it was during the blitz that I was there—'that little Island I am convinced, on a properly representative program of a World Immigration Budget (or what we now call Displaced Persons) will take in 150,000— or in any event will match the great United States, up to 150,000! The boss turned to me—I thought I had done a good job—and he said, 'A hundred and fifty thousand to England; 150,000 to match them in the United States; pick up 200,000 or 300,000 elsewhere; we can start with a half million of the oppressed.'

"I came back in about a week. My wife was with me. Roosevelt turned to her and said, 'Margaret, can't you get me a Jewish Pope?' He said, 'I can't stand it any more. I've got to be careful that when Stevie Wise leaves the White House, he doesn't see Joe Proskauer on the way in.' He turned to me adding: 'Nothing doing on the program.' I said, 'What's the matter?' He said, 'We can't put it over because the dominant vocal Jewish leadership of America won't stand for it.' And I said, 'It's impossible. Why?' He said, 'Well, they're right from their point of view. The Zionist movement knows that Palestine is, and will be for some time, a remittance society. They know that they can raise vast sums for Palestine by saying to donors, "There is no other place this poor Jew can go.' 'But,' said Roosevelt, 'if there's a world political asylum for all people irrespective of race, creed or color, they can't raise their money. Because the people who don't want to give the money will have an excuse and say, 'What do you mean there's no place they can go but Palestine? They are the preferred wards of the world.'

"I could scarcely believe it. I didn't want to believe it. That a bit of chauvinism and nationalism among a few leaders of the Jewish organizations of America could defeat an over-all haven for the oppressed of Europe. I said, 'Let me test it out.' I went to friends of mine, without mentioning the British people I had spoken to, without mentioning Roosevelt—I laid down this grand dream, this great plan—of the world joining together to give relief to the people pushed around by Hitler.

"I assure you that I was thrown out of parlors of friends of mine. And they said very frankly, and they were right from their point of view, 'Morris,' they would say, 'this is treason—you're undermining the Zionist movement.' I'd say, 'Yes, maybe I am. But I'm much more interested in a haven for a half million or a million people—oppressed throughout the world.' "

Thus Zionists were sufficiently powerful to shut off every other movement for succor elsewhere other than Palestine. Their leaders refused the offer of ships to bring the refugees in the Black Sea ports to temporary havens in North Africa. Even the pathetic victims of persecution in the forlorn Displaced Persons Camps, longing for some small measure of security, wanting simply to get out, praying for escape, were not free from coercion. Many of them who wished to go elsewhere than Palestine were forced to stay in the camps and there discriminated against unless they yielded to Nationalist pressures to go to Palestine. Rabbis and laymen were compelled to silence or compromise, or cajoled and lured into support. Many Gentiles, some of them men in public life, serving as a Zionist front, have made a good living from subsidies received by them for pro-Zionish lectures, addresses and appeals. One by one groups and organizations yielded. Even organizations traditionally opposed to Jewish nationalism, like the American Jewish Committee, joined in the clamor for a Zionist state in the futile belief that they could control Jewish nationalist activity or at least put a break on its extreme manifestations. The Union of American Hebrew Congregations was pulled into the orbit of the nationalists, following similar commitments of the Conservative and Orthodox religious groups. The religious Mizrachi fled their ground and became among the most pugnacious of protagonists for the state. Thus the nationalists achieved their goal—the re-nationalization of the Jew in Palestine in the State of Israel. But contrary to the assertion that all would be well when the state was born, greater and more delicate problems present themselves to American Jews now that Israel has been established.

We witness today a complete transformation in the thinking of Orthodox, Conservative and Reform Jews about Judaism, about their relations to Jews in Israel and to Jews and non-Jews the world over. The individual Jew must submit to the discipline of nationalist thinking; all right and wrong, good and bad derived from whether what is said or done promotes the welfare of the Jewish people in the State of Israel. The shift in emphasis from religion to nationalism is one of the reasons for the present-day secularization of Jewish life. Judaism, the God-centered faith, with its profound call to social justice for all men, has become Palestine-centered and nationalistically slanted. Judaism, the nationalists say, is but one facet of a culture that is decadent and distorted unless it be Israeli-inspired. There is even a new vocabulary which proclaims the cult of 'Jewishness.'

What is this cult of 'Jewishness' of which so much is heard? What does 'Jewishness' mean? In Israel today it means the rejection of the use of the Yiddish language, although there is a great literature in this hybrid tongue. It means placing a ban on Reform rabbis and their work, only now, reluctantly, slowly and with great difficulty being lifted. Under the Citizenship Law enacted by the K'neseth it means putting the American Jew in a special and privileged position vis-à-vis Israel and making it necessary for an American citizen if he would avoid military service in Israel to declare his American citizenship on entering the country; it means putting the Arab minority in the position of second-class citizens, legislation which has called forth condemnation even in some Zionist quarters. Jewishness in our country means to some a violent orthodoxy and the promotion of parochial schools for Jewish children; to others it means singing folk songs of eastern European origin with a ghetto intonation. The current concept of Jewishness is in essence separatist and foreign and has replaced "frommichkeit," piety. As a result, the life of American Jews has lost many of the old sanctities. Instead of "Kiddush ha-Shem," the traditional injunction to sanctify the name of God through righteous conduct, there has been substituted "Kiddush ha-Am," a glorification of the Jewish people. Jewish idealism is measured in terms of nationalist activity, folkish ceremonial and Israeli interest more often than in terms of the spirit.

The nationalists declare that if there be such a thing as a Jewish mission in the world, it cannot be dissociated from the State of Israel. They have not hesitated to use pressures of all kinds, even intimidation and character assassination, against those who oppose them. Jews wanted to help their brethren and did not concern themselves with the implications of Jewish nationalism. Our leadership, rabbinical and lay, intellectually and otherwise, was nationalist for the most part, or compromised or was silenced. There was not enough stamina in pulpit or pew to say: this thing shall not be. There was not enough willingness to oppose the nationalists and take the consequences.

Only one organization, the American Council for Judaism, raised its voice in opposition to the nationalization of Judaism and Jewish community life. Because of the stand it has taken, the Council and its members are maliciously represented, vehemently assailed, called anti-Israel, anti-Semitic and pro-Arab. If there were such a thing among Jews as an effective excommunication, they would most assuredly have been excommunicated. This sturdy band of some twenty thousand men and women have accepted the injustice of which they are the victims in good spirit. Their warnings were not heeded by a generation that had been conditioned by Zionist propaganda. But the Council has spread information where before was ignorance, and it has brought some degree of clarity into the confusion which characterizes contemporary Jewish thinking and practice. Most of all, it has set an example of moral courage in the dreary wasteland of nationalist conformity. Many who describe the Council as fanatic are beginning to see what nationalism has done to Judaism in Jewish community life.

What is the nationalist program? To infiltrate and conquer the American Jewish community, to control all its institutions and organizations—educational, philanthropic and religious; to charge them with Jewish nationalist philosophy and to bind them ideologically, psychologically, and emotionally to the State of Israel. Mr. Daniel Frisch, President of the Zionist Organization of America, in an address "The Zionist Organization at the Crossroads", given in January, 1949, presented a four-point program for organized Zionism here and abroad. Among other things he said, "... Zionism is a synonym for Jewish life. And nothing is as important in Jewish life as the Jewish school. Whoever holds the key to the Jewish school holds the key to the Jewish soul and the Jewish future. To leave that key in the hands of the Sunday School alone is to court disaster. . . . I have a feeling that the American Jewish community will soon arrive at the inevitable conclusion that the all-day school . . . is the only solution to the problem. Our future leaders . . . will come from such schools . . . which are Israeli oriented and which are at the same time not unmindful of the American-Jewish mileu. . . . I consider it an axiom that every Zionist worthy of the name give primacy to the national welfare over the partisan interest of any group in Zionism in America or in Israel. . . . We must be extremely vigilant against the infringement of this all-embracing principle of the supremacy of the national weal over group interest."

At the Sixty-first National Convention of the Zionist Organization of America held in Miami in October, 1958, Mr. Abraham Redelheim, elected President at that Convention, appealed to Zionists all over the United States to capture the Jewish communities controlled by non-Zionists. He told American Zionist leaders that the leadership in many Jewish communities in America now lies in the hands of people who have a negative attitude toward Jewish national and cultural needs and also toward the vital problems of Israel. The only way to deal with this problem, he said, is to adopt the slogan suggested by Theodore Herzl, the founder of political Zionism sixty years ago, "Capture the communities," and control them in the interest of nationalism. He continued, "Zionist penetration of the Jewish community, Zionist education in all its facets, Jewish history and tradition, Hebrew language and literature, aliyah and chalutziut, the place of the State of Israel in the comity of nations and the part it must play in the unification of the Jewish people all over the world, the vigilance and awareness by our Zionist family, particularly in these United States, to preserve the integrity and security of our creation —the Jewish State." (*The American Zionist*, November-December, 1958)

At the same convention Rev. Dr. Mordecai M. Kaplan, a leading and liberal Zionist, a distinguished theologian who founded the Reconstructionist movement (a courageous attempt to re-think the philosophy and practice of orthodoxy in Judaism), gave an important address in which he outlined a new program for American Zionism. He called for "The reaffirmation and reconstruction of world Jewry as a religio-ethnic trans-national people, united by a common history and a common spiritual destiny" and he stressed "the supreme importance of the centrality of Israel to the survival and enhancement of the Jewish people throughout the world." In "Religion and Nationalism," an article in the November, 1958, *Jewish Newsletter*, he wrote, "The next step which, I hope, Zionism will make is to redefine and reaffirm the status of the Jewish People as the bearer of the Jewish religious civilization, and to accept formally the fact that its intention is to continue as a transnational People, with a religious civilization which is to be lived out in full in Eretz Yisrael, and only in cadre form in the Diaspora."

Dr. Kaplan believes that this is the Jew's unique contribution to the idea of nationalism. Jewish nationalism is religious or must be chastened by the injunctions of religion. Dr. Kaplan and the Reconstructionists believe in a sort of mystical union between nationalism and religion. This is at least some slight advance over the political emphasis in Jewish nationalism.

I accepted a similar position during the years when I was affiliated with the Zionist organization. I wrote in *Seed of Abraham* (Century Co. 1930) in an essay on Herzl: "Our present day world conceives of nationalism in political terms, in terms of empire and sovereignty. The Jewish conception of nationalism is different. Jewish nationalism seeks the opportunity to express the soul of the Jewish people in terms of institutions, culture and civilization. This is the new conception of nationalism which the Zionist movement expressed and which holds a lesson for our world."

However, in 1938, having seen Jewish nationalism at work among Zionists here and in Palestine, I wrote in *Common Ground* (Liveright, 1938): "Jewish nationalism today is different. Its emphasis is political. Its methods are political. It is a Chukath ha-

Goyim. . . . The nations of the world can understand a world religious community, and accept it; they will never understand or accept a world community whose nationalism is maintained not only at its political center but throughout the world. This is especially true in the present state of world tension, when national unity is the first essential for national self-preservation."

The nationalist philosophy of Dr. Kaplan as well as its practical application in our country is unacceptable to many American Jews. He proclaims "my nationalism is a cultural thing." The facts of contemporary life make it impossible to distinguish fine shades of meaning in the term nationalism. Nationalism means only one thing in the public mind. It means political allegiance. You cannot take a current word, give it your own particular meaning different than that usually denoted by it and expect the public to understand. Furthermore, American Jews should be familiar with the practical application of Dr. Kaplan's nationalism. He spells it out in detail in his monumental volume *The Future of the American Jew*. (Macmillan, 1948). He envisions a tightknit community "united in a body of democratically elected representatives" of local community councils and of national Jewish organizations representing inter-communal causes. Such a body would "represent the ethical nationhood of Jewry in its American aspect. . . . It will administer, face the economic problems in so far as they are group problems, focus all social services, and provide organs of defense against antisemitism. It will . . . provide a sociological framework within which it will be easier for Jews to live as Jews, function as Jews . . ." Spelled out eloquently and definitively in this extraordinary book, Dr. Kaplan's philosophy and its application here would make Jews a self-isolating, self-segregating group, set apart from their fellow-Americans. It would ghettoize the American Jewish community. His philosophy and program could lead ultimately to a special legal status for Jews and a return to the conditions of mediaeval times.

Dr. Kaplan acknowledges that "what was wrong with the tribal and national religions in older times was their exclusiveness and arrogant egoism. . . ." That is just the point I make. The tendency of Jewish leadership here and in Israel, lay and rabbinical, is exclusive, tribal and arrogant and yields no place to an interpretation of Judaism as many American Jews understand and want to practice it.

It has been charged that my interpretation of Judaism abandons the world kinship of Jews and would isolate Jews from their brethren. This is a misunderstanding of my position. I do not believe that any Jewish community can cut itself off from the trunk of Jewish life without impoverishing itself. I have never denied the brotherhood of Jews. I believe that to be a Jew and a follower of Judaism means something more than acceptance of a set of religious and ethical principles and social obligations. There is a mysterious *plus* which makes us more than a denomination. We are the inheritors of a religio-cultural tradition. The birthland of Jews has a place in that tradition. For some it has a larger and a different place than for others. What I object to is the attitude current among the majority of Jews today which gives primary place to the State of Israel—not the homeland—and the present tendency to base one's loyalty to Judaism and Jews on acceptance of Jewish nationalism as interpreted and applied here and in Israel. This is just the point Dr. Kaplan ignores.

Nationalist educators start with the proposition that it is impossible for the Jewish child to lead a normal Jewish life in the non-Jewish American environment. But what is a normal Jewish life? Is it to fill the child with an ever-present consciousness of being different from his fellow Americans, with an unhappy belief that he will always feel the stings of anti-Semitism, that there is nothing he can do about it except fight it? Is it to feed his pride with nationalist values by way of compensation? This is being done in hundreds of Sunday schools and afternoon Jewish schools and in youth groups in all parts of the country. Under the stimulus of nationalism, the movement for Jewish parochial schools is growing. No organization dealing with our Jewish youth is free from the taint of nationalist propaganda. Nationalists have infiltrated into positions of responsibility and leadership, so that many textbooks used in the liberal congregations are designed secretly or openly to emphasize the nationalist philosophy, to glorify Israel, to play on whatever feelings of insecurity our youth may have, to mold their tender minds to the Zionist pattern. Folk songs and dances vie with the religious musical responses; the flag of Israel often stands with the Stars and Stripes in the assembly halls and sometimes on the altars. The separatist propaganda of the nationalists is found not only in our Sunday and other schools, but on the campuses of our colleges and universities. It is aggressively promoted in the Intercollegiate Zionist groups; it manifests itself frequently in Hillel Foundation activities where the spirit of divisiveness and self-isolation is often fostered. Hundreds of Jewish youth are now being trained in Israel to be sent forth to the Jewish communities of the world, particularly to the United States, to indoctrinate, propagandize, evoke emotional responses and develop pyschological ties to Israel among American Jewish youth.

It is obvious if these influences are not stopped by active opposition, walls will be built instead of bridges; our Jewish children in America will grow up unmindful of their American heritage, sharing in it only with hesitation and doubt, not trusting their childhood friends, filled with a sense of ineradicable difference, perhaps even nursing their disappointments with a chauvinistic pride which already has made some of them insufferable. Any psychologist will verify the fact that when a young mind is subject to such conditioning, instability, discontent and lack of inner harmony may well develop psychic disorder. And yet many of our lay leaders who are not Jewish nationalists themselves lend their names and influence to this distorting, poisoning, and totally un-American conditioning. I cannot believe they realize what they are doing.

It will be said by the nationalists: "Ours is a program of cultural education. Jewish nationalism will of course be kept in Palestine and we do not want it here." Doubtless some who say this are sincere but official Zionism here and in Israel has no

intention of limiting Jewish nationalism to Palestine Jewry. Their
program of Jewish education is designed to maintain the nationalist
philosophy among American Jews under the guise of promoting
Jewish culture. These Zionist organizations here are tied in with
the Palestine sources of nationalist propaganda.

Suppose every other minority group in the United States did
the same thing. What would happen to democratic America?
It would be fragmented, splintered, shattered into a score of
groups, all self-conscious, all hyper-sensitive, all desperately attempting to preserve their various identities; suspicious of each
other, overreaching each other and in the end perhaps fighting
each other. If American Jews do not actively oppose Jewish
nationalism here, we shall find ourselves reduced to a tight little
community bound together by ties of blood, and linked by romantic attachment to an Israeli state which consumes our material
and spiritual resources.

The diversion of the major funds raised by American Jews for
nationalist causes has brought about a starving of our Jewish
institutions here. The general chairman of the campaign to promote American Reform Judaism told a group of six hundred
Reform rabbis and lay leaders that of the more than $130,000,000
contributed by American Jews in recent years for health, welfare,
refugee, and overseas programs," considerably less than five million
dollars is being made available for institutions that have as their
goal the preservation, strengthening and advancement of Judaism."
In pointing to the growth of the Reform movement, whose con-
gregants number now more than a million, he said, "We can take
no comfort in growth if at the same time we are being starved
financially." (New York Times, October 14, 1958.)

The New York Federation of Jewish Philanthropic Agencies,
serving 116 hospitals and welfare agencies and caring for seven
hundred thousand people of all races and faiths each year, found
it is necessary to state in a two-page ad in the New York Times
January 12, 1959, that it faced a critical financial emergency which
might force a reduction in its essential humanitarian services.

Meanwhile, the United Jewish Appeal announced a campaign for a special fund of a hundred million dollars in addition to its 1959 campaign for a hundred and five million dollars to take care of the expected large influx of Jewish immigrants from eastern Europe to Israel. Perhaps the proposal of Rabbi Braude of Providence, Rhode Island, which appeared in the journal of the Central Conference of American Rabbis, should be given earnest consideration: "I propose also that the United Jewish Appeal follow the pattern whereby the American government allocates money in Israel. The American government has a special commission which selects agencies or enterprises deserving aid and gives direct subventions to such agencies or enterprises. The United Jewish Appeal ought to do likewise.

"The welfare of the people of the State of Israel requires new and imaginative procedures in the expenditure of the monies of the United Jewish Appeal. We Jews in the United States should not continue indefinitely the signing of blank checks for the government of Israel. My concern is primarily for the welfare of the people of the State of Israel and, for their sake, I believe firmly that the time has come for American Jewry to determine both the manner and the purpose for which the funds we give are spent. The sooner we do so, the better."

Certainly there is a limit to the generosity even of American Jews. The recent immigration from Rumania was probably part of the well-known Soviet strategy to keep the Middle East pot boiling. Suppose the Russian dictators decide to release the three million Jews in Russia, as the Israeli Premier, Ben Gurion, has surmised. Israel would be faced with an impossible practical problem and American Jews with a financial burden they could not possibly bear. A reappraisal of this situation is necessary and American Jewish leaders cannot recognize it too soon. This is not a problem for Jews alone. It is an international problem. It should be made the concern of the United Nations.

A recent study undertaken by the American Council for Judaism reveals the startling centralization of Jewish organizations here;

that they are dominated by nationalists to advance nationalism. Community centers' programs are designed to make for "a heightened ethnic consciousness . . . the Seventeen Presidents Club which includes the heads of most of the major organizations of American Jews, it is now admitted, was organized and is controlled by the Jewish Agency," a nationalist group closely related to the government of Israel. The so-called Presidents Club engages in political pressures and presumes to speak not only for the organizations represented in the group but for all American Jews. This was too much even for the Zionist editor of the Chicago *Jewish Sentinel*, Mr. J. I. Fishbein, who declared in the February 7, 1959, issue of his publication that the membership of the organizations had not been consulted, Mr. Fishbein stated, "We have not been asked for our opinions on what should be done; no one has reported back to us as to what has been decided; the local groups have no autonomy of their own except to rubber stamp national decisions; and the national bodies are primarily influenced by two or three strong personalities."

Mr. Jon Kimche, Editor of the *London Jewish Observer and Middle East Review*, last year made an extensive tour of the United States in order to observe the Jewish scene here and was shocked by the trend among American Jews toward self-ghettoization. He also comments pointedly, "All the principal American Jewish movements are negative; they are either anti-defamation or anti-discrimination or anti-Arab. American Jewry is beset by a demonology which is constantly fighting. It is defensive all the time. It is worried by what others say so much that it has completely forgotten what it wants to stand for. It is always against something, never for. It is always answering what someone else has said. It appears as anything but the pulsating intellectual giant it could be."

To summarize: Dare American Jews present themselves to their fellow citizens as a self-segregating community building walls around themselves, and differing from their fellow Americans in strange ways other than those enjoined upon them by their religious faith? Dare they do this at this time when the most earnest educators are searching for methods and techniques to develop sympathy and understanding among groups in America; when our best minds are engaged in an intensive effort to bring about harmony and cooperation among Americans of all colors, creeds and cultures?

But most important of all to me is this: shall the universal insights which have been our glory—a consciousness of God's reality and a solemn call to duty, freedom and brotherhood, prophetic insights which are our chief claim to any influence in the world—shall these become but memories in Jewish life?

If we do not lift our voice in condemnation, we condemn ourselves as moral weaklings before the awful majesty of our religious traditions. Will you tell me that Judaism has no vocabulary with which to speak to the world except the vocabulary of nationalism; or that Judaism has no message of righteousness to proclaim when men in political and economic life make compromise with evil and link arms with corruption; or that Judaism has no other word to cry aloud except Israel, Israel, Israel, in this hour when freedom is assailed here and everywhere by the very voices which presume to speak in its name?

In this situation I suggest: let non-nationalist Jews concern themselves with the sort of Jewish education that children receive; let them get on religious and Sunday School boards, examine the textbooks, familiarize themselves with who is teaching, with what is being taught, and how it is being taught. Non-nationalist Jews should insist that the presentation of the non-nationalist position be made in the classes and assemblies and at as frequent intervals as the nationalist position. Non-Zionist literature should be supplied and distributed, debates held where the material is not slanted and the judges are fair. Congregational authorities as well as parents should be made to see the problem. The same policy of critical appraisal should be employed in the programs of all our organizations, our social and philanthropic agencies, our community councils and our Jewish community and temple centers.

In the light of all the factors in the situation, this is the least that wise non-nationalist leadership can say and do.

We have discussed the philosophy of Jewish nationalism and the program of the nationalists. Let us now consider the methods of the Jewish nationalists.

If the Jewish nationalist movement runs its full course there ultimately will be little democracy and less religion in American Jewish life. American Jews will be under an authoritarian and oppressive regime which will stamp out all freedom and mould the American Jew of the next generation to the nationalist pattern.

There is a disinclination in some Jewish quarters to speak on this question openly because it is said: This will create anti-Semitism and give ammunition to the Jew-hater. Why wash dirty linen in public? I reply: it is false to assume that our fellow Americans are not familiar with what is going on. The Jewish Information Bureau reported on July 27, 1958, an increasing interest by non-Jewish groups and individuals in Jewish religious, philanthropic and cultural activities in the United States. Gentile and Christian resentment of Zionist philosophy, program and methods is growing stronger. This was indicated in the results of a recent survey of Christian periodicals made by the Anti-Defamation League. It is better for a Jew to talk about them and show concern about them, than by silence to condone them. It is better for the Jew to condemn them openly than that Gentiles should whisper about them. What is wrong in letting friendly non-Jews know that many Jews are troubled and that we need their help? There are unworthy aspects in the life of all groups here. Concealment and secrecy are not the normal American way. To be silent, to pretend that these abuses do not exist and that our fellow Americans are not acquainted with them is to play ostrich. Naturally Zionists will resent such effective opposition. But for non-Zionist Jewish organizations to blame individuals and organizations which have the courage to discuss these questions openly and frankly is gratuitous. It is characteristic of the moral cowardice which has vitiated the integrity of Jewish leadership in America. To blame such organizations and at the same time to continue to cooperate with the nationalists and Zionists in the forlorn hope to curbing their extremism is pathetic self-delusion. We dare not be neutral in this effort to free American Jews from those whose methods are in principle no different than the methods of Torquemada, Hitler, Franco and the Russian Polit-bureau.

For the first time in American Jewish life the Jewish nationalists entered politics on a Jewish issue. They have called upon candidates for public office to support Zionists and Israeli foreign policy —or else. Threats were made to oppose any candidate or party which opposed Israel or was lukewarm or non-commital. Even those Jews who were not nationalists but were moved only by sympathy for their brethren were drawn into the American political scene *as Jews*. The non-Jewish community was subject to similar pressures and intimidation. Things have come to a pretty pass in our country's life when an American citizen is voted in or out of office, not on the basis of what he is or stands for, but on whether he supports the position of Jewish nationalists.

The Zionists rightly or wrongly have already evoked in some quarters the feeling that regardless of the general welfare they would bend our nation's policy to the presumed advantage of a foreign state. In the past such procedure by other groups in relation to Ireland, Spain, Germany and Russia has generally been looked upon with distaste, suspicion and disapproval.

Jewish nationalist activities caused anti-Semitism in normally friendly quarters. Economic boycotts against American firms, such as that conducted against certain cigarette manufacturers who, because of the economic pressure exerted by the Arab states, stopped selling in Israel, or the campaign against the American Express Company for closing its office in Jerusalem because of lack of business, are misguided efforts with possible unforeseeable boomerangs. It is questionable whether such activities will help Israel. It is unquestionable that they do harm to Jews here.

The opposition by the joint committee of nine Jewish bodies including *all* the rabbinical bodies, the American Jewish Congress and The National Community Relations Advisory Council to Christmas observances in the schools is inept, unwise and in the long run bound to evoke anti-Jewish attitudes. It is interesting to note that the American Jewish Committee, an organization which has frequently cooperated with Zionist bodies, is not involved in this activity. These groups call upon Jews to oppose such observances on the basis of "the separation of church and state." It is accepted that majority rules in a democracy and minorities have rights which must be respected. In the struggle to free itself from domination by both the divine right of kings and by the church the western world devised the way of democracy. While it is true that majority rule was the compromise effected, it is equally true that the rights of the minority must be recognized. This does not mean, however, that a minority can override the emotions and traditions of the majority. It might be well for Jewish organizations dominated by the nationalists to bear in mind the inconsistency in a position which demands in this country separation of church and state but in the Zionist state accedes to the demands of an autocratic orthodoxy. It should be added, of course, that in Israel there are protests against such outworn hierarchial claims. The Christmas spirit apart from its theological implications cannot be outlawed. The season in its general sense is beautiful and universal. It civilizes, at any rate, for a brief period of time. Its spirit is in the air, it is contagious. It is presumptuous for any Jewish organization to demand that the spirit of Christmas be ignored in our public schools.

The anti-Semitism caused by such Jewish nationalist activities seems to be forgotten by organizations which call upon Jews to spend considerable sums to defend them against anti-Semitic attacks. In this connection it should be noted that a startling change has taken place in the attitude of the Christian religious press toward Israel and toward Jewish attitudes toward Zionism. From unreserved sympathy expressed in the earlier years, the majority of church and denominational publications are frankly critical of Israeli policy and of Zionist activities here.

In their publicly avowed aim to dominate the American scene,

Jewish nationalists have employed tactics characteristic of all authoritarian movements. A young lawyer in Los Angeles accepted the invitation of the local non-Zionist group to serve on its board of directors. Several days later he phoned to say that Zionists had brought such pressure upon him that he was forced to withdraw his acceptance in order that he might earn enough to support his wife and family. A bond broker in Boston was told in innumerable phone messages from Zionists in his clientele that unless he resigned from the American Council for Judaism they would take their business away from him. A doctor in a mid-western city suffered the same treatment. A clothing manufacturer who needed linings was informed by a house with which he had done business for years that if he would contribute to the Zionist cause he could get all the linings he wanted; if not, he could get none. These are not isolated instances. They represent the pattern of Jewish nationalist activity in this country. Several months ago the Free Jewish Club was started in New York by a group of distinguished Yiddish writers, professional and businessmen who, refusing to follow the nationalist party line, were subject to all sorts of abuse and discrimination. The *Menorah Journal*, the most distinguished publication of its kind in the United States, until very recently was in part supported by subventions from the Welfare Funds in various cities. The *Journal* publishes significant articles of philosophic, religious, literary and artistic interest. Its contributors represent a Who's Who of Jewish scholars and writers and its readers represent the cream of the intellectual and cultivated Jews. When its editor, Dr. Henry Hurwitz, published papers critical of the machinery of philanthropy controlled by the United Jewish Appeal and the Welfare Funds, the nationalists in various cities forced the discontinuation of support for the magazine.

A hidden Zionist censorship tried to prevent the publication of any news or views not pro-Zionist and pro-Israel. It was nearly one hundred per cent effective in the American Jewish press whose editors, reporters and owners are ardently nationalistic. It is only within the last few years that American citizens can get the facts about the Middle East Arab-Israeli situation. One brave and independent voice in the wilderness of sameness has been that of William Zukerman, Editor of the *Jewish Newsletter*. Zukerman's effort at objective reporting of Zionist and Israeli news brought vicious attacks on him and efforts, fortunately unsuccessful, to silence him. I would point out in passing that there is more freedom to differ and to criticize their government among the citizens of Israel than there is among American Jews to criticize the Zionist-nationalist dominated American Jewish scene. It is both startling and important to note a manifesto published recently in Israel by a group of Sabras, youth born in Palestine. *Lebensfragen,* a Tel-Aviv weekly, in October, 1958, carried an account of the new organization in an article by I. Mamter, a staff writer: "For those who still identify the Israeli State with Zionism, it will certainly be of interest to be acquainted with the new anti-Zionist political organization recently formed in Israel, composed not of immigrant 'Galut' Jews, but of Jews born and reared in this country—Sabras." The thinking of this organization mirrors the sentiments of wide circles of Israeli youth: ". . . they stand on the proposition of freeing the State from Zionist domination: of abrogating the privileged status of the Jewish Agency and of all other Zionist funds and institutions which are carrying activities parallel to those of the [Israeli] government.

"In place of the existing Zionist regime, they want to institute a democratic secular regime which will materialize the full equality of rights of the Arab population [of Israel], as well as the complete separation of Religion from State.

"They do not believe that the Jews in the rest of the world constitute a separate nationality *with regard to the peoples among whom they live.* [They regard them as only a religious community.] ". . . while the Zionist regime enslaves the State (of Israel) to foreign Zionist purposes, it enslaves simultaneously the Diaspora world Jewry. The myth that the Jews of the world constitute a nation whose center is in Israel and that all Jews are obligated to pay allegiance to Israel places world Jewry in a complicated, precarious position. . . . Back of the facade of that myth [that all Jews in dispersion constitute a single nation] Zionism succeeded in creating throughout the Western dispersion a totalitarian apparatus compelling Jews to subordinate themselves unreservedly and uncritically to the Zionist regime in Israel—by threat of social ostracism, by the refusal of burial rites, etc. [In short], the authors of the Manifesto accuse the Zionists of sabotaging the [true] relationship between the Hebrew nation [as being formed currently in Israel] and the Jews in the rest of the world. . . ."

That such provocations as I have described here should take place without strenuous opposition is distressing enough, but even more deplorable have been the enervating and degenerating effects of Jewish nationalism on the religious life of American Jewry. Wherever possible presentation of the non-nationalist point of view is prevented not only from pulpits and before Jewish audiences but before general audiences. In many congregations Zionists threatened resignation if the non-Zionist point of view were voiced by the rabbi. The result has been unworthy compromise or the destruction of free pulpit utterance. Many rabbis yielded rather than split their congregations under Zionist pressure. Some refused to compromise and the resulting disunity caused schisms and in some instances rupture in these congregations. The failure of our rabbis and laymen to oppose such tactics is gradually undermining the integrity of our religious life. One may ask what does it mean to maintain the unity of a congregation at such a cost? What respect can the institution merit whose lay leadership imposes such sanctions or whose rabbinical leadership accepts them? Meanwhile, of course, in those places where the nationalists are in the majority, the feelings and sentiments of non-Zionists more often than not are ruthlessly overridden. The long range result is inevitable—the loss to Judaism of many of its most representative constituents. Eventually large groups to whom not peoplehood, not nationalism, but religion, Judaism, is of primary importance, will gradually pass out of our temples. Such Jews will not subject themselves or their children to nationalist education and propaganda.

This is an old story in Jewish life. Again and again the best among us has fled or been driven from us by the limited and the constrained. They refuse to be pulled back and down to the parochial and particular. Their Judaism in thought and practice was universal, not national. Thus the self-isolating little community persisted, rejecting the laws of normal social behavior, until another cycle of persecution began.

The nationalists suffer from the illusion that they are preserving people and faith by insistence on difference. On the contrary, they are prolonging the epic sorrow of the seed of Abraham. I make no plea for Jewish self-destruction, but for a brave reassertion of the universal faith that is Judaism and a confidence in the truth and strength of that faith to preserve the best that Judaism and the Jew have to offer to the world.

Certainly for the moment the Jewish nationalists hold the reins. They are continually asserting that on the question of support for the State of Israel all Jews are united and that only an inconsequential minority opposes them. Perhaps that is true. It is true that all Jews are united in the matter of support for education, health and general welfare of the Israeli population; it is also true so far as reasonable support for new immigration into Israel, housing, reforestation and the economic development of the country are concerned. It is not true that all Jews are united where the support demanded enters the area of Israel's political propaganda and interests.

Now that the Zionist state is a fact and the implications and dangers of Jewish nationalism here are so apparent, I believe that Jews and Gentiles who hitherto have supported the nationalists out of humanitarian impulses should draw the line against further encroachment of Jewish nationalism in this country. They should distinguish between Zionist politics and Jews in need; between uncritical political support of Israel and the strengthening of educational, cultural, welfare and other activities in Israel. This realization cannot come too soon.

Jewish nationalism and its influences are not in the Jewish

tradition. It is a new role for the Jew who has ever been concerned with the good of humanity and contributed to the enrichment of science, art, literature and social gain wherever he lived, to be suddenly preoccupied with his own survival. It is unthinkable that he should not realize that the survival of any group in the world depends upon the survival of freedom and democracy in every corner of the world and that unless all citizens of all nations unite to secure these blessings for all, they will be safe for none.

Now is the time for Jews and non-Jews who have been browbeaten and badgered by Zionist and nationalist pressures to speak out in the name of American democracy and decent human relations.

This controversy among Jews has nothing whatever to do with whether Jews come from Poland, Lithuania or Pinsk, or whether they come from Paris, London or Philadelphia. It has everything to do with a choice between ghetto and freedom, between idolatry of the state and worship of God, between Jewish "blut and boden" and that far horizon envisioned by Isaiah and Lincoln.

Men of moral courage, Jew and Gentile, should raise their voices in every community against the abuses of the Jewish nationists. If this were done it would not be long before the unholy spell would be broken, the intimidations would cease, the American Jewish community and the American scene would rid themselves of these baneful and subversive influences.

What is to be done? There is still time enough to save American Jews and Judaism from the domination of the nationalists. We need only a band of determined men and women who are willing to take up this challenge. Example is contagious. One man who asserts himself can save a community. One community can serve as an example to many others. American Jews must rid themselves of living under the pall of fear of the nationalists. There must, in short, be a revolt of individuals and community leaders against Jewish nationalist dominance of our American Jewish life! Wherever Jewish nationalism lifts its head in our country, there must be firm, clear and uncompromising opposition to it.

The time is here to carry the American Jewish spirit forward out of emotional ghettos so often forced upon us, so often pathetically accepted. The spirit of America and the spirit of Judaism are harmonious. They strengthen and reinforce each other. We can think and act and live here as Jews and as Americans without the violation of any Jewish values. We must pour money into the crowded Jewish centers of population; open new synagogues, religious schools, educational centers, character developing instutions. We must proclaim the spiritual verities of Judaism today in the light of the problems of contemporary life; preach a Judaism that is vital, that touches life intimately on all its sensitive surfaces; a Judaism that appeals to the mind, that gives comfort to the heavy-hearted, that offers challenge for social betterment.

You may ask me, "What is a Jew?" In answering, I would ignore all the pilpul of the theologians, the obsessions of the racists, and put the answer in simple, understandable contemporary terms. A Jew is a person who accepts the heritage and faith of Judaism, whose life and conduct manifest the ideals he professes, and who feels himself a kinsman in the world family of Jews. He will live justly and compassionately with all men as he, himself, walks humbly with his God. And what is Jewishness? It is the spirit of the psalmist and his sensitivity to the presence of God in all things; it is indignation at wrong and cruelty and the unswerving will to make them right; it is the consciousness that we belong to a fellowship chastened in suffering, and whose message the world needs for its healing and its well-being; it means rejoicing in the religious heritage of our fathers, observing form and ceremony and festival and holy seasons as poetry and symbol, but holding fast to the ideas they represent, and practicing them in our daily lives.

These are the things I would choose as representing "Jewishness" rather than the glorification of land or people or state! I said twenty-five years ago, "To me, the universal insights of Judaism and their social implications must dominate Judaism in this country or the faith of our fathers will become an empty shell of folkist ceremonial, as the Jewish nationalist philosophy would make it to be." Events since then have strengthened me in this conviction.

For what is Judaism?

Judaism is a series of religious insights into the meaning of the world and life. It is an attempt to answer the ancient questions: What is man? What are his duties and responsibilities? It proclaims the mystery of God who is creator and Father and to whom man is responsible. These insights are universal; but Judaism's insights are not only speculation and belief; they are not in the clouds but have to do with the very stuff of life, with man's dilemmas, his temptations, his problems, his strange potentialities for evil and good. Therefore, Judaism's universal insights in the area of faith are complemented by its universal ideals in the area of conduct, in its injunctions as regards human relations.

Man is under obligation to seek truth in thought and to pursue freedom, righteousness, justice and brotherhood among men. Judaism took these universal ideas and clothed them in the poetry of form and ceremony naturally wrought out of the experience of Jews, in order to discipline the life of the Jew. In Judaism there was always a consciousness of a common brotherhood of faith. It was the recognition that all Jews shared the universal religious insights, however differently they interpreted them and were committed to their preservation and their promotion. Until it felt the impact of Jewish nationalism, Judaism, born out of the vision of the Old Testament prophets, evolving through the generations after the destruction of Jerusalem by the ancient Romans, was conceived as a universal religion. It was so presented by Jewish saints and scholars and rabbis to their fellow Jews and to the world. The Jew as a religionist is in the line of those inspired prophets who preached in Palestine centuries ago their message of social and spiritual regeneration; in the line of the psalmists whose profound insights led the world to prayer; in the line of that ethical and moral tradition from which sprang Catholicism, Protestantism and Mohammedanism. No philosophy of nationalism will be the instrument of Jewish salvation either here or in Palestine. No pride of military conquest in Palestine—not even the redemption of some hundreds of thousands of Jews on the soil of Palestine in the State of Israel—can becloud the fundamental issue: Are Jews to be a people like all other peoples and Judaism a national religion with Jews living throughout the world emotionally tied to the Zionist State and drawn into its international dilemmas, or are Jews and Judaism to be exponents of the universal insights which are the essence of Judaism and its special and enduring contribution?

But, I have been asked, who will defend the State of Israel against its enemies, and maintain what has been achieved there? Will you abandon the state and its people? Certainly not! Help for our brethren abroad? Of course! Relief to the limit of our capacity. But we dare not let the needs of Jews blind us to the larger drama on whose world stage we Jews play indeed a lesser role. Our sorrow is but one segment of the world's sorrow and it must make us cognizant of the sorrows of other groups and of all kinds and creeds and classes and colors. Our sickness cannot be isolated from the sickness of the world nor can it be healed by us alone. We are but one of the casualties in a war for the redemption of humanity and that war will go on.

Perhaps history will record some gain in the establishment of the State of Israel. But history will also write into the record of this time that it was then when Judaism and the Jew cast away their right to speak with moral authority—when they elevated Jewish nationhood above human brotherhood.

The nationalist may declare that what we say—Judaism is a religious community—has been said by countless other religious communities. It is not essentially Jewish. Other men believe in God. Other men believe in social justice. What is there essentially Jewish in such ideas? I answer, they are the heart and inspiration of Judaism! The very asking of the question indicates the degree to which they have turned away from the springs at which we were nourished. To fail to recognize this and to turn elsewhere for

Jewish values is to miss the way, to choose the chaff, to sell our birthright.

Judaism cannot accept as the instrument of its salvation the very philosophy of nationalism which is leading the world to destruction. Shall we condemn it in others but condone it for ourselves? In the face of the brutalizing nationalisms of our times, Jews must proclaim the universal message of Judaism. Not the blood cult, state cult of nationalism in all its manifestations; not this is our message to a tired, stricken world, but this, the message of the still, small voice which amid all the din and thunder of the centuries has never been stilled: one humanity on earth as there is but one God in the universe. This is the burden which history and our tradition have laid upon us.

Let us not chain the exalted values of a universal vision to narrower confines, but give the vision free rein to find perhaps its highest expression and to make its greatest contribution to human brotherhood. Nationalism will not save the Jews here or in Israel. Judaism will save the Jews in Israel and everywhere else. My own conviction is that Jews today must stand firm in their devotion to the idea of a religious community, consecrated by its heritage of a literature, an historic experience and a deathless hope, not for itself, but for all mankind.

CHAPTER SEVEN

The Meaning of Judaism

> In Judaism faith is . . . the living consciousness of
> the omnipresent, the feeling of the nearness of
> God, of his revelation which manifests itself in
> all things, of the divine creativeness which lives
> in everything . . .
> It is the affirmation of the meaning and value of
> life . . .
> In Judaism, love towards God is never a mere feeling,
> it belongs to the sphere of the ethical activity of
> man . . .
> Judaism bears witness to the power of the idea as
> against the power of numbers . . .
> Judaism by its mere existence is a never-silent protest
> against the assumption that the multitude can be
> greater than right, that force may be the ruler over
> truth . . .
>
> LEO BAECK

THE great theological systems in many respects are similar to
the metaphysical systems, in that while the basic ideas have for
the most part persisted through the centuries, the emphases
change. From the time of Plato and Aristotle man has been concerned with the problems of existence and ultimate reality, the
apparent and the real, the spiritual and the material.

Kierkegaard's Protestant Existentialism and Marcel's Catholic Existentialism, distinguishing as they do between existence and essence, the world as it is and the world where all problems are resolved, are but contemporary rounds in the incessant struggle of man to reconcile what he is with what he hopes to be. Each retains not only the universal religious idea but also the schematisms and vocabulary of its own traditional theology and in this respect Maritain's criticism of Karl Barth referred to earlier has some truth. Kierkegaard's explanation of Grace and Redemption are Kierkegaard's interpretation of grace and redemption; and Marcel's explanation of Grace and Redemption are Marcel's interpretation of grace and redemption; the one a Protestant, the other a Roman Catholic interpretation of these two fundamental ideas. And they are true for Protestant Kierkegaard and his followers as they are true for Roman Catholic Marcel and his followers. But no matter how profound or original their ideas may be, they remain, to the uncommitted mind, interpretations.

In Judaism also, Orthodox and Conservative and Reform leaders suggest certain principles the acceptance of which constitutes a good Jew. But these principles likewise are only human interpretations, with all the limitations that implies. Thus there are differences between Orthodox and Liberal Judaism, just as there are differences between Orthodox or Evangelical Christianity and Liberal Christianity. For Liberal, unlike Orthodox Judaism, does not speak in terms of dogma. It speaks in terms of principles and these principles are universal. True they are matters of faith, a faith which the Liberal Jew should constantly submit to the critique of reason. But even Liberal Judaism takes the position that there is a point beyond which reason can not lead the inquiring mind. At that point faith steps in and, covering itself with the mantle of humility, declares these universal principles are the essence of truth and reality, the ideals which should govern human behavior.

Thus far I have distinguished between religion and the Religions. I have pointed out the wholesome self-examination in which Christians and Jews are engaged and the importance of reason as an instrument of revelation. I have referred to tendencies in all the religions to revert to an authoritarian position which rejects reason and often brings the Religions into conflict with the state. It is only fair that I submit to the critical mind my own faith as a Liberal Jew.

This chapter does not pretend to be a full presentation of Judaism. I shall discuss some of the general ideas of Judaism; some of the religious insights which Liberal Judaism shares with Christianity, as well as the Jewish interpretation of these insights which differ from the Christian interpretations. Finally I shall discuss the place of Jesus and the concepts of atonement and redemption in Liberal Judaism.

Let it be understood that I speak with no authority except that which love for Judaism, belief in it, sympathy with Jewish life everywhere and a long ministry have given me. I speak for no one save myself and out of what study and observation have brought me to accept. What I have said and what I now say will not satisfy all Jews. It is but one man's judgment.

Judaism is not a race cult. Its followers are not all of one blood or one cephalic index or one race. There are black Jews in Ethiopia and New York; yellow Jews in China; brown Jews in India. It does not elevate its devotees above the peoples of the earth nor pander to their sense of pride by telling them bedtime stories of an alleged superior genius.

Neither is it a national religion, appealing only to Jews. Through historic circumstances, and because of forces working within it, and pressures on it from outside, the Jewish people are the bearers of Judaism; but Judaism is a religious philosophy of life, universal in its scope. It proclaims ideas about God, about life, about human relations. Judaism is a universal religion and welcomes to its fellowship all men and women who accept its teachings.

Golden threads intertwine in Judaism to weave the pattern of man's thinking and conduct. The psalmist's longing for God, the prophet's passion for social justice, the priest as the conservator of the traditions and values of life, and the rabbi as teacher and inspirer. Judaism teaches that all derives from God—all life, all good—and that man's highest purpose in life is the imitation of God. All the love the Christian gives to Jesus, the Jew gives to God. Jews are taught to love God with all their hearts and all their souls and all their might, and to love their fellow man as their brothers. All is God . . . the wonder and the majesty of the world without! He is there! The mystery and beauty of the world within? He is there! This is to cultivate the individual, to sensitize him, to give him a sense of humility as he ponders God's greatness, and at the same time a sense of his own dignity because God needs him as he needs God!

Judaism cannot conceive of God and man's relation to Him only in terms of the individual. Prayer, formal ceremony, public worship, sacred literature, all of these are indeed needed. But the reality of God is made manifest when they who believe in him express that belief in human relations. All the wrongs and unrighteousness of human life, the wickedness, the greed, the unholy ambitions of men, groups and nations which lead to misery and war, these are the concerns of Judaism. Just as Peter sitting by the fire and warming himself is a reminder to Christians of the challenge to bestir themselves as soldiers of Christ, so Judaism proclaims to its followers: God does not desire prayer and incense, sacraments, liturgies and ceremonies alone. You who believe in Him, take up the struggle to protect the weak, to shield the innocent, to restore to the disinherited their portion, and to set truth, righteousness, justice, and brotherhood as the very foundations of society. Spirituality in the individual life; compassion, justice in human relations—these are the foundations of peace.

Judaism enjoins its followers: "Seek the peace and welfare of the city where ye make your habitation, for in its welfare is your own." There is no duality of interest between Judaism and the state, no conflict between the sovereignty of the state and the obligations of Judaism. Judaism does not seek nor claim any special area of interest that conflicts with that of the state. Judaism declares to its followers: "The law of the land is your law."

These are some of the general ideas of Judaism. Because of these ideas, Judaism has made a number of original contributions to the thinking of our time.

The universal ideals of Judaism are at the core of the Anglo-Saxon tradition, whose interpreters and creators drank deep from the wells of living water in the Old Testament. Bible personalities were the intimate associates of England's leaders, the inspiration of their private and public conduct. The ethical injunctions of the Bible influenced the political and economic development of England. "To your tents, O Israel" was the battle cry of Cromwell and his followers. In our times the late G. K. Chesterton, certainly no friend of Jews or Judaism, discussing the then Sir Rufus Isaacs, later Lord Reading, declared it would be better for him to appear with robe and turban as befits the Oriental he was. Chesterton seemed to despair that his countrymen would ever understand the real nature of Jew and Judaism because he said the Anglo-Saxon still stands transfixed with wonder before the mystery of the Jew.

The United States was founded by men and women who, moved by Judaic ideals of justice and freedom, came here with the burning desire to build a nation whose policy and economy would embody the prophetic teaching. Calvin Coolidge was profoundly right when he referred to the "Hebraic mortar" which was the very foundation of our national heritage. The unity proclaimed in the Sh'ma* may have been to the Jew only heroic assertion of a theological principle; but its influence was not confined to the realm of ideas only, nor limited to one group. It flowed over into conduct. God's unity and Fatherhood implied the unity of mankind. Each generation had the responsibility to reinterpret truth and to understand God. This made for renewal and continuous survival. It made the faith a living thing. It isolated Deity in the awful loneliness of perfect holiness, but it brought Him closer to men in the

* Hear oh Israel, the Lord our God, the Lord is one!"

intimacy of personal quest. Political and economic organizations and all human relations felt the impact of this deathless vision of Judaism. The struggle to realize it still goes on, and the years immediately ahead will test the strength, the sincerity, and the moral courage of the followers of Judaism.

Judaism has made original contributions in three areas. One: Judaism proclaims the idea of progressive revelation; two: Judaism has achieved a singularly clear balance between authority and freedom; three: Judaism enunciated a unique conception of community.

According to Liberal Judaism truth was not revealed fully and finally at Sinai. Judaism rather emphasizes the evolutionary nature of God's unfolding plan. Not through one personality or one group at a given moment in history did God reveal Himself to man, but God continuously manifests Himself through the good and the righteous of all peoples and in all times and places. The persistent iteration of this truth had immeasurable influence on non-Jewish thinking, particularly Protestant thinking. It evoked a critical attitude toward dogmatic assumptions. It made for flexibility, for openness of mind—what William Ellery Channing called "the free soul." Once man is touched by this idea, not only is his religious attitude transformed but all his thinking and, ultimately, his conduct. It naturally follows that the drive for truth, the desire to yield to its leading, colors his attitude toward the economic and social problems of the day.

Judaism has achieved a singularly clear balance between authority and freedom. The sovereignty of God underpinned Jewish ethical and social ideals; it gave them dignity and power. It was man's duty to interpret the divine. But human insights differ. Liberal Judaism, realizing the inability of man utterly to comprehend God in the absolute completeness of His reality, was humble before the inscrutable questions of human life and destiny. "The Torah (Jewish teaching) speaks the language of man." Whatever one says is limited by the limitations of mortality.

There are many today who are willing to sacrifice their freedom for the serenity which often comes to those who believe in an authority which proclaims: In me are light and truth and redemption. Judaism utters a mighty protest against man's relinquishing to any man or group of men his obligation under God to seek truth. Judaism is a protest against the rising tide of theological, political and economic arrogance which would deprive man of his proud heritage to "seek truth and pursue it." Not only the unhappy circumstances of Jewish life but the essential nature of Judaism itself prompted the moving prayer of the synagogue liturgy for the destruction of the "dominion of arrogance" from the earth.

Judaism enunciates a unique conception of community. "All is God's," Judaism declares, "in the heavens above and on the earth beneath; there is none else!" Out of this central conviction rose Judaism's unique idea of justice. Charity is praiseworthy, but in Judaism it was commanded not only as an attitude of the generous and sympathetic heart; charity is a matter of justice, a sacred obligation upon the Jew because he is a member of a religious community. From this conception of charity, as far back as Talmudic times, came the beginning of communal organization among the Jews, which took care of the needy, the sick, and the underprivileged. In no small degree the Community Fund idea derives from this religio-social philosophy of Judaism. And not only in the Community Fund idea and organization has the influence of Judaism been profound; it has been and is being felt in the elevation of standards of social work. "You were strangers in the land of Egypt" has been the recurrent refrain of our liturgy and ceremonial. Every generation should conceive itself as having been strangers in the land of Egypt; for "not with you alone did I make this covenant" but with all the generations that followed. Such conceptions sensitized the Jewish spirit. The late Joel Blau put it eloquently in one of his essays when to the twin conceptions of Judaism, the Fatherhood of God and the Brotherhood of man, he added a third, "the Homehood of the World." This is Judaism's unique conception of community.

Our America is the setting in which these ideas of Judaism

have flourished and expanded. They have profoundly influenced American thinking and conduct. The American conception of the separation of Church and State, perhaps the supreme contribution of this nation to political and social theory and mores, offers the larger horizons congenial to the universal ideals of Judaism.

Our present dilemmas and the problems ahead are real and pressing: capital and labor, worker and management, white and colored, Jew and Christian, old resident and newcomer. We need all we have of faith and courage as we move into the future years. The faith of the fathers with its emphasis upon progressive revelation, with its insight into the relation between authority and freedom, with its insistence upon the idea of community consciousness, responsibility, and obligation, is still a youthful, vigorous warrior for the unrealized prophetic dream.

As I see it, what is needed above all among American Jews is profound conviction. American Jews must have conviction about their faith, about themselves, about their function in the world. There has been too much drift without compass, too much willingness to compromise with wrong, and too little courage to oppose it. We Liberal Jews of America have been men of little faith. What Jews need is vital leadership, conscious of its purpose, undeterred by misrepresentation, criticism and abuse, devoted to Judaism as a living faith, rich in cultural and artistic creativity, an inspiration for noble personal living and social usefulness. We need an American Jewish laity inspired by such a faith, courageous as it faces the dilemmas of the present and confident of its future. We need an American Jewish community which has thought through its problems from an American Jewish point of view, knows what it believes and where it is going, and moves forward in a unity that transcends its differences, serving not only itself and its brother Jews everywhere, but its country and all mankind. In America there is the possibility of the most thrilling revival of Judaism perhaps in all Jewish history.

Unlike traditional Christianity, traditional Judaism enunciates no salvation-conditioning dogmas. It does not promise: Believe this and you will be saved. Nor does it threaten with: Unless you believe this, you will not be saved. The idea of salvation as conceived and developed in Christian theology is foreign to Judaism. Salvation in Judaism, so far as the individual is concerned, meant a rescue from danger or from a threat to one's life; in later times it meant a redemption from evil or from sin. But the threat of danger was always in *this* world. In authoritative Judaism there was no implication of the individual's persistent anguish that he would be punished after death for sins committed in this life. The salvation and redemption of Jews as a group were similarly salvation from oppression, redemption from persecutions. This is particularly evident in those early periods when Jews were under Roman rule. The Messiah in Jewish thought was he who would life the yoke of the occupying power so the Jew would once more be free. In medieval times when the fate of the Jew depended upon the whim of the prince, priest, or potentate, redemption naturally came to mean the "return" to the land of the fathers, where life would be more secure and "exile" and wandering would cease.

For the Jew today the idea of redemption has many practical angles. He must insist upon his right to live anywhere as a citizen enjoying the fullest rights of citizenship and he must be protected in that right. He will endeavor to find homes in friendlier lands for those of his co-religionists the roots of whose lives have been destroyed. He will aid those who wish to return to Israel.

But as I see it, redemption for the American Jew means something more. It means redemption from tribalism and an espousal of that universalism for which the world yearns and which is so essentially Judaism. It means a re-thinking of his Jewish position in terms of his relation with his fellow Americans; it means that he throw out all the vestiges of the years of oppression which have scarred his soul, limited this thinking and set him apart in ways other than those imposed by his faith. It means that he fulfill the high challenges of his heritage in the integrity of his daily conduct. It means that social justice becomes for him not only a phrase from the prophets or a pious prayer in the synagogue but a vivid impera-

tive, a solemn injunction he must observe. It means that in the face
of persistent prejudice he keep faith in man, in God and in the
ultimate victory of right.

It means his release from every shackle of irrationality and
superstition. Judaism was not designed to imprison but to release
him. His Judaism is not a jail; it is a gateway. It is not a burden
to be borne; it is a banner on which is inscribed, "For truth, for
freedom, for brotherhood." and under which its followers may
march forward toward the redemption of the world!

Unlike traditional Christianity, Judaism has never developed a
systematic theology. In one sense this may be a weakness; but in
many ways it has been a very real source of strength. The Jewish
mind differed in this respect from the Greek mind much as the
French mind differs from the Anglo-Saxon. The former approaches
a problem with a penetrating rationality, a disciplined logic: the
latter approaches a problem rather more intuitively. The former
drives through to an inevitable and inexorable conclusion; the
latter muddles through to an unpredictable though usually satis-
factory resolution.

Profound difficulties arise in any effort to build the structure of
a systematic theology in Judaism because of the differences of opinion among the rabbis, whose ideas often contradict each other.
What should be accepted as authoritative Judaism? When faced
with this dilemma an extraordinary and apparently illogical solution was found in the rabbinical phrase: "Both are the words of the
living God." In other words Judaism in its broadest reaches was
sufficiently inclusive to give hospitality to opinions which apparently cancelled each other out. For example, "All is foreknown
and man has free-will" satisfied the scholarly for generations. Perhaps the secret of the matter lay in the nature of the Jewish mind
as well as in the character of Judaism. It was sufficient to believe
that God is and all else followed. Why wrestle with the impossible
task of trying to formulate the details of the divine schematism
if, even at the end of the search, any conclusions reached would
always be limited by the limitations of man's mind and none

could say what was complete and final truth? With all due respect to the sincerity of the theologians of other faiths and to the majestic architecture of their thinking, I rather prefer the simple formulations of Judaism and its inherent humility to such grandiose systems. Other theologies necessitate the acceptance of certain basic presumptions which more often than not are matters of faith, incapable of proof, but without which the entire structure, so arduously built, falls to the ground.

Unlike many forms of traditional Christianity, Judaism has no ecclesiastical system. It has no hierarchy which stands in some special relation between God and the people. The congregations are autonomous, with the weakness which comes therefrom, and the rabbi is the teacher. "Rabbi" in Hebrew means "my teacher," and when the followers of Jesus called him "Rabbi" they meant one set apart as "teacher," by reason of certain gifts of mind and spirit which lifted him above the crowd. Judaism has not sought, nor does it seek, any temporal authority in semblance or symbol. It is a living religious tradition, expressed through voluntarily organized, self-governing congregations, for the enrichment of the personal lives of its members by worship and religious education and, through them, the promotion of the general good.

Because Jews do not consider Judaism a final and complete revelation of God's will but rather one of many insights of man in his search for God, Judaism must be reinterpreted in each generation as man's knowledge reaches out to further and widening horizons. In Reform Judaism the principle of tradition has come into its own. Liberal Jews have dared to apply the principle of evolution to their faith and followed it to its logical conclusion. They must see to it that this perennial spring of renewal does not dry up. They must see to it that Liberal Judaism does not degenerate into an orthodoxy of its own and that it recognize a persistently revealing divine spirit. For having once made its escape from the power of a static tradition, Liberal Judaism might itself become inflexible in its own tradition and become but "a remembrance of things past." It must be true to its own essential genius.

Not the ideas of Reform nor the externalities of Reform are most important, but the principle of Reform: the principle of a tradition, adapting, adjusting, always alive—embodying the universal Jewish ideal in thinking and conduct according to the knowledge and need of the times.

Such a conception of tradition points to the majesty of the past. It regards with reverence what the past has done and has given. It offers gratitude to the past, recognizing that all we are, we are by reason of what the past has conserved. Yet it declares that to accept blindly, to follow unthinkingly, is to stop the flow of revelation. This definition of tradition calls us to account not only before the authority of the past, but before the bar of the future. It declares that we in the present are not only the conservers but the makers of tradition.

Such an interpretation is gripping and dramatic, as well as scientific and reasonable. It summons men to effort and enlargement. It is one of the glories of Judaism; it constitutes one of its chief claims to the discriminating mind.

While I was still a rabbinical student, an essay of David Hume on the theology of Christianity made an unforgettable impression on me. It revealed the essential character of any theological system, not only Christian; the imperious demands it makes in the name of faith, as well as the unavoidable challenge to reason as the "great corrector." Hume puts the matter simply and with brave but brutal frankness.

Adam and Eve fell because of their sin. All the generations born after them were conceived and born in sin until a merciful God, realizing the necessity to redeem His creatures, appeared on earth in the form of a man who was born miraculously, lived, suffered, was crucified, and redeemed by his death the sins of all the world. This theological schematism, it should be remembered, is based upon the literal acceptance of the Garden of Eden story.

Perhaps this condensation of Hume's is an over-simplification and does not do justice to a conception which has claimed the devoted faith of millions, the consecrated intelligence of theologians and philosophers, and the death of many martyrs, and which has produced libraries of books for the thoughtful and the faithful. But it does point up the dilemma in which the critical intelligence finds itself, a dilemma with which the fearless, liberal spirits in Christendom have persistently struggled.

You may say, "How can Jesus be other than divine, for no mere man could have done the things he did?" And yet to assume that Jesus actually did the things the Bible says he did is just as gratuitous as the belief of an orthodox Jew that the waters did part and the Hebrews did walk across the bed of the Red Sea, or that Moses did write down the Ten Commandments at the dictation of God. Must we accept as literally true all these accounts written down years after the events they described took place? How much misinformation there is, even in our day of radio, television and immediate communication. How much more misinformation there must have been in those earlier days!

The greatness of Judaism and Christianity does not depend upon miracles. It is a greatness inherent in a sublime insight. Jesus' greatness is not explicit in the miracles he is reported to have performed. It is implicit in what the story of his life evoked in the lives of men.

Dr. Charles Clayton Morrison, brilliant Protestant leader and for many years Editor of *The Christian Century* delivered an address some years ago in the Chapel of the University of Chicago on "The Crisis in Christianity." He made two points: first, that the traditional Christian emphasis on salvation of the individual soul through contact with the personality of Jesus has outlived its usefulness; and, second, that the emphasis of Christian teaching and practice must be shifted to the prophetic, to the social, to the idea of the salvation of society. He holds the latter to be the essential Christian doctrine. The address was prophetic. It should be pondered not only by Christians but by Jews.

I should like at this point to give my own thought about Jesus. It represents only a personal view. Many Jews will agree; many will disagree; and others will dissent violently. I trust that no Christian will be offended.

It is difficult indeed to dig beneath the mountains of propaganda and controversy and unearth the core of truth about a personality like Jesus who has been the center of discussion among Christians for twenty centuries. Passages like that where Pilate speaks: "I am innocent of this blood," or like this: "His blood be on us and our children," are generally recognized as spurious. They were written down later as propaganda by men whose business it was to further belief in Jesus, The Christ who died to save the sins of the world. Ideas die hard, and when these ideas are the foundations upon which great religious and theological systems have been built, they die even harder. The problem is well-nigh insuperable when it is obviously to the advantage of the religious institution which is founded on them to continue to promote them.

Yet truth shall march on. Humanity will lift itself gradually out of error and superstition into enlightenment. Jesus, the man-made God must in the end give way to Jesus the God-made man! The gradual triumph of reason and free critical inquiry over unreason and uncritical acceptance is written in the unfolding book of man's tireless search for truth.

It is true that many Jews denied he was the Messiah. It is true that a group of powerful Sadducees and Pharisees combined to turn him over to Rome. But it is equally true that the earliest followers of Jesus were Jews. It is true that to many Jews of that day, though he was not God, he was the eagerly looked-for, long-awaited Messiah. It is true that Jews cared for him; that Jews followed him; that Jews walked with him along Via Dolorosa and up Golgotha's heights. It is true that Jews wept for him and took his body tenderly down and gave it decent burial. It is true that after his death, as before it, Jews were his first disciples. It is true that the first Christians were Jews and that in the synagogue the first sermons of the daughter Religion were preached to Jews. It is true that those who first bore the cross of Jesus were Jews. It is also true that the Jewish people have borne the cross along the Via Dolorosa of the years, and have faltered up Golgotha all these weary centuries.

Jesus believed he was Messiah, the son of God, in a different and peculiar way. He claimed to speak in the name of God. Other prophets of Israel had spoken in God's name but they had said: "Thus saith the Lord," or "The Word of God came to me." But not so Jesus. He seemed to identify himself with the message. "No man approacheth the Father save through the son." He suffered Peter to call him "Lord."

Why? Did he really believe these things? Perhaps so. And because he conceived of himself in a special sense as the son of God different from the usual and current understanding of the term, the leaders of the time, who felt themselves obligated to maintain the worship of the one spiritual God, lent themselves to his execution.

While the Jew apprehended God everywhere, he localized Him nowhere. The embattled history of Israel is the struggle against idolatry, against man-made deities, whoever and whatever they may be. For this reason no saints or images, no pictures or art such as made so colorful the religious monuments of mediaeval Europe, are found in the Synagogue. The God-intoxicated Jewish prophets claimed to be only messengers of the Divine, His spokesmen. But here was one who claimed a unique relationship with God, and whose disciples later claimed that he was God, who came to earth miraculously born, who suffered and died to save the world from the sins which had been inflicted upon it because of the sin of the first Adam. What Jesus' followers did and said of him in the later years justified the fear of the Jew that the unity of God was jeopardized. How could the Jew, to whom the idea of the divine unity was the highest expression of the religious life—how could the Jew accept him either as the Messiah or as God, as the intermediator or the Saviour? "Hear, O Israel, hear all mankind, the Lord our God, the Lord is one!"

I often wonder what Jesus himself would say if he could hear and see the things that are spoken and done in his name. What would he think of the tortures that have been inflicted, the martyrs that have been burned, the wars that have been fought by those who presume to act in his name? The simplest, humblest, and tenderest of men, what would he feel if he witnessed the pomp and show and power, often the vindictiveness and prejudices of those who say they represent him and act for his glory? What would he think if he heard the declaration that outside a particular belief about him, a particular form of worship of him, there is no salvation? How he would scourge the hypocrites and scribes and Pharisees of today in church and cathedral and synagogue! How he would plead for faith and brotherhood in the name of God, the Father!

When he died, most selfless of men, he died as a Jewish martyr; not the first nor yet the last of many Jewish martyrs. He sprang from our loins. We could have understood him. But the controversies of the past dimmed our eyes to the beauty of his life. His protagonists have claimed more for him than he himself could or would claim. They have made of him a god and worshipped him.*

* * *

The Christian world stood outside the ghetto wall it built around the Jew and looked at him with critical, often with hostile eyes. In self-defense, the Jew built a wall around himself and gazed in wonder or sadness or hostility at those who in the name of their Christian religion had so strangely used him and Jesus the Jew. Breaches have been made in the wall on both sides, but portions of it still stand and it is sadly ironical that there are Christians and Jews who would build it still higher today.

But the problem of the Jew is also the problem of the Christian. The Jew will not come forth into a world which only condescends to tolerate him. His pride will not let him do this. He will go back to the warmth of his own fireside. The Christian must meet him half way, not with the evangelist's passion to convert him but with the hand of fellowship.

* From the author's *Common Ground* published 1938 by Liveright Publishing Corporation.

For the Jew does not want Christianity. The followers of the Jew of Nazareth must understand that on this there can be no compromise. The Jew in coming into the world will be himself— he will live as a Jew. As a Jew he will best serve the world.

To me Christianity and Judaism seem to complement each other. Two principles stream through all creation, now side by side, now parting, but always returning one to the other, merging and fortifying each other. They are the female and the male. Christianity represents the female principle, with its emphasis upon the mystic, the tender, the compassionate. Judaism represents the masculine principle, with its solemn call to duty, its over-weaning sense of responsibility to God. Christianity elevates love as the highest principle. Judaism affirms justice as the noblest goal. But in Christianity, justice stands at the side of love; and in Judaism, love stands at the side of justice. We need the two for the enrichment of our civilization.

The idea of atonement is one of the central themes in both Christian and Jewish thinking. "For God so loved the world, that He gave his only begotten Son, that whosoever believeth in Him should not perish, but have everlasting life." (John 3:16) Down the centuries rings the mighty call to repentance and redemption. And millions of Christians renew their faith at Christmas as they tell the story of Jesus' birth, and at Easter, the strange story of the Resurrection.

In Judaism, as in Christianity, the idea of atonement grew out of one of man's deepest needs—his yearning for reconciliation with himself, with his fellowmen, with his Maker. At first this need expressed itself in the form of sacrifices. A goat, bearing the sins of the people, was thrown over the cliff. But as Judaism in its evolution advanced, it purified and spiritualized the idea of atonement. It abandoned, together with the idea of vicarious atonement, the sacrifice of the scapegoat, and created instead the Penitential Season which rises to its climax in the Day of Atonement, when the Jew is called to self-examination, to self-criticism, to repentance, to reconciliation with his fellowman and with his God. On that day every Jew, no matter how far he may have wandered from the faith of his fathers, feels a strange tug at his heart. Memories covered over with the dust of wasted effort and dulled by time and circumstance, rise from the depths of his being. The grandeur of the day-long ritual measures up to the majesty of the theme. It speaks to him of God's forgiveness, His everlasting love.

Strange insights come to the lonely and the suffering. As human beings, as men and women, Jews turn with simple, childlike faith to God at this season. "Forgive us, Father"—we say in the ancient liturgy—"for the wrongs we have done, for the mistakes we have made, for the hurts we have caused, for the things we should have done and have failed to do." As a religious community we pray: God grant us strength and forbearance and courage. Grant us the confident faith of our fathers. We pray not for material things but for a greater measure of Thy spirit, that our lives may testify to the truths we proclaim and witness to Thy glory.

We turn to the God of our fathers. We must have no part in the ruthless selfishness, the brutal oppressions, the sanctimonious hypocrisies that lightly cover pusillanimous compromises at other people's expense, and betray man's hard-won-freedom. The voice of an ancient teacher rings with persistence in our ears: "Put not your trust in princes." We Jews have yielded our blood in every land, endured auto-da-fé pogrom and rack and pyre and exile and wandering. For what? For a conviction. That conviction could not, cannot be bought. It is not for sale in the market place. Strange insights indeed are those that come to the lonely and the suffering.

In the midst of the disillusionment and cynicism of the times, we know we must play our historic role as religious teachers. Behold us, an ancient people! *God is*. At the heart of the universe is law, a law of the spirit. That law is righteousness and loving kindness. These are the foundations of civilization. No man or nation can flout or deny this law and endure. Man cannot compromise with evil. In its conception of atonement Judaism reaches beyond the individual, beyond the particularistic. Its sublime universalism achieves fullest expression.

The need for atonement reaches around the world. We are, all of us—Jew and Christian—all the peoples and the nations of the earth, guilty of complicity in the sins of society. Dishonesty, selfishness pay dividends of distrust, discontent, corruption, and dissolution. There is no vicarious atonement for the wrongs men inflict upon their fellowmen and the sins nations commit against each other. The only atonement is to tear away the delusions, the short-sightedness, the selfishness, to see ourselves as God sees us! Then go forth to do better. Atonement summons all to repentance. It calls man to link his will with God's will so far as he can conceive of that will and thus achieve the redemption of the world.

Wars are fought and armistices signed and peace comes for a time. But there is another struggle in which there can be no armistice. It is the struggle against hypocrisy and for sincerity; it is the struggle against tyranny and for freedom; it is the struggle against brutality and for humanity. There can be no surrender to those things which degrade men and the nations and which destroy their integrity.

Christianity and Judaism have so much in common. Accepting the mind and will and love of God as realities in the mysterious universe, both seek to inspire man with confidence, to comfort him with hope, to elevate him with the faith that what he thinks and feels and does has value in building God's Kingdom on earth. While Christianity and Judaism differ in their interpretations of the religious insights, both lift the banner of a universal dream.

It is important therefore that Christians and Jews respect not only the symbols of their Religions but their substance, that they reverence not only the forms of their Religions, but their reality.

When Christians and Jews do this, and only when they do this, will they begin to understand what Moses and Jesus were talking about.

CHAPTER EIGHT

Bridges — Not Walls

Behold, how good and how pleasing it is for brethren to dwell together in unity.

PSALM 133

UNTIL these latter years, no one thought much about religious prejudice or the irreligious competition among the Religions, except the scoffer, the agnostic, and the atheist. They stood on the side lines and said, "See what the believers and the faithful think about each other, how they talk about each other, and act toward each other. If that's religion it's not for us!" The criticism is justified. While we religionists talked about salvation by conduct as well as by faith, it was the faith that most frequently mattered. To most of us, of course, *we* had "the truth, the whole truth, and nothing but the truth," and that truth was the means of salvation. Many of us drew a charmed circle about ourselves and those who believed as we, and said in effect, "*We* are the people, and outside us there is no salvation." The good Lord had been very nice to us to let us in on the secret of salvation, and although the uninitiated might be very good people, we had some sneaking doubts about them and their ultimate destiny, for we knew that redemption was given unto us but were not so sure about the fate of those others. We did not give much "mind" to the conduct which must in the end justify, defend, and prove the truth of our convictions. There were exceptions in all groups, but for the most part, a bland condescension or indifference or hostility marked our attitude toward those whose faith differed from our own.

When we consider the bitter historic memories, the profound dogmatic differences among Protestants, Roman Catholics, and Jews, the deep emotional attachments evoked by all the Religions, we cannot hope to refashion the relations between them in a single or even in a number of generations. When we add to these things the shortcomings of religious and lay leadership in all the groups, the temper of the times, and the fact that we are dealing with one of the most powerful of human feelings; when we see how wide is the chasm between the various branches within Judaism and Protestantism, despite the contemporary movements in both of them for ecumenicity; when we contemplate the cultures, the nationalisms, the languages that divide Roman Catholics, when we consider all these things, we should not be too disappointed that the kingdom of God has not been built in our time. Ecumenicity among the Protestants still has a long way to go, and Peter stands aloof from Paul, insisting on his prerogatives; while Jews unite to care for their sick and dependent, and contribute generously to Palestine reconstruction, gaping canyons of intellectual and emotional differences divide Yemen from the Ukraine, Manchester from Mobile, and Paris, France, from Paris, Kentucky. But progress in interfaith understanding has been made, singular, unprecedented, undreamed-of progress, in the last quarter century, and at least a pattern has been established, which does represent advance.

So far as the Christian-Gentile attitude toward Jews is concerned, the old saying, "First we preyed upon them, then we brayed at them, now we pray for them," has contemporary manifestations in all three categories. This much thus far has been accomplished: when some Gentiles prey upon Jews today, widespread disapproval and generous sympathy are evoked among most Christians; when they bray against Jews, more frequently than not they receive the Christian condemnation they deserve. As for those who pray for the Jew, sincere prayer never did anyone any harm and, as it mellows the Christian attitude to him, it may cause the Jew to be, as he should, more critical of himself, his thinking, and his conduct.

It takes two to make a contract, and when only two parties are involved, agreement of some sort is often easily reached. If the number is more than two, the settlement is more difficult to achieve. The will to sympathetic comprehension of another's point of view is the first axiom of mutual understanding. If one or several or all minds are closed, tight, and inflexible, it is well nigh impossible to find a basis for compromise and cooperation. These simple truths are fundamental in interfaith work. But because the goal is in the distant years and the road is hard and long, is no reason why the Religions and all men and women of goodwill should not try to walk it together. Man's earth does move around the sun of all the hopes and dreams that ever lifted his mind and heart. During these last twenty-five years definite progress has been made in the work of inter-faith understanding.

The findings of modern psychology and sociology seem to indicate that prejudices are rooted in the character of the individual or group. We must ask what are the reasons for the fears, frustrations and sense of insecurity which find expression in attitudes of prejudice, in acts of discrimination and in physical persecution. As Rev. William W. Simpson of the British Council of Jews and Christians writes in his pamphlet, "Where Two Faiths Meet" (1955): "In the attempt to answer this question the sociologist and the psychologist, the economist and the politician all have their parts to play. But for the Jew, no less than for the Christian, the ultimate answer must be a religious one." I agree heartily with this statement and it is in this spirit that one must consider the possibilities for and the limitations upon cooperation between Christians and Jews.

When shall we understand and accept what Moses and Jesus were talking about? When shall we learn to tear down the walls and build instead the bridges? Goodwill is not a one-way street and our lives lose much that will enrich them when we build walls between ourselves and our neighbors.

The forces against religion and the Religions are elemental and brutal. They rise out of the deep past of primitive man. We have not yet disciplined or chastened them enough to make the stark and driving passions behind them work constructively. They lie hidden, silent and dormant within us, but they can come to the surface in one swift, conquering moment and destroy us. These primeval instincts fulfill themselves in and are strengthened by the more lately developed loyalties to nation, creed and culture. Their imperious demands override all differences, and unite a group or a people in a passionate will to power. Other forces consciously prevent fulfillment of the universal, ethical teachings of church and synagogue—such as the economic power of undisciplined wealth or of class conscious, undisciplined organized labor. This sort of power often seeks to control politics, to dominate the press and the other media of communication, to condition education so that its own ends will be served, and to fashion custom and law to fit its purpose. It is jealous, uncompromising. To it religious institutions are not instruments of salvation, symbols of the goals which the saints and dreamers have set for mankind. It supports the organized Religions only when the Religions support it. When the Religions dare to oppose it, they become an enemy who must be pushed aside. If our eyes have been open to what has gone on in the world these last years, we must have seen how designing men and groups have used not only man's selfishness and fears but his most unselfish feelings to play people off against each other, to attack them separately, to divide and, in the end, destroy them.

These evil influences are found not in one group only. They are not in the ranks of capital and labor alone; they are not in British, Russian, Chinese or American imperialism alone; they are not in Roman Catholic, Protestant, Jewish or Muslim groups alone. They are to be found in all groups, nations, and Religions. In politics and economics, they make for totalitarianism of the right or the left, for Fascism or Communism; in the field of the Religions they make for clerical totalitarianism. It is the task of real religion—Roman Catholic, Protestant, Jewish and Moslem—to reveal them for what they are, enemies of true religion, and oppose them. These enemies are within the organized Religions themselves, dividing them from each other at the very moment when each needs all its physical resources—numbers, substance, influence —all its spiritual resources—faith, conviction, loyalty—to combat the ancient and modern enemies that would pervert them, use them, and then wipe them out.

Protestantism closely followed the pattern set by the Roman and Eastern Orthodox churches. It tended to rely on the state. In most places except in the United States and in Switzerland, the tradition linking the state and the church is of centuries-long duration. Britain, while recognizing an Established Church, maintains the equality of all Religions before the law. While separation of church from state was won in France over a hundred years ago, the ambitions of conservative clericalism are still factors to be reckoned with in French politics. In Prussian Germany the Lutheran Church was linked with the state, as in Bavaria was the Roman church. In Poland and Russia, up to recent times, the union of church and state was almost complete. It was broken as the Communist influence penetrated, controlled and now tries to destroy the influence of the Roman church.

When the Religions relinquish their conscience to the state or seek to win place and power in the secular and temporal orders they lose the right to speak with moral authority.

These tendencies are manifest also among Jews: they are manifest in Israel where the influence of orthodoxy has brought about a reversion to theocracy; they are manifest in the United States and elsewhere, where acceptance of the primacy of Israel is openly urged by Zionists as the highest duty of the Jew. But just as the vast majority of American Protestants and Roman Catholics realizes that the basic fight is against the powers of darkness and evil, so the vast majority of American Jews realizes the nature of the struggle;

as Paul of Tarsus put it in his Epistle to the Ephesians: "For our wrestling is not against flesh and blood but against the principalities and the powers, against the rulers of the darkness in the world, against spiritual corruption in high places." (Chapter 6, Verse 12)

Although uncertainty surrounds the months and years ahead, this is certain: that none can work more effectively for the regeneration of American life than the men and women in our churches and synagogues. Our progress would have been greater, had we not brought strange idols into our shrines. We have given our loyalty to Baal when it should have been devoted to the living God. Perhaps we have not understood the role which religion should play at this time, or, understanding it, we have not had the moral courage to insist upon it. Perhaps we have been servants of institutions rather than witnesses for the Living God. The test of true religion is not creed, it is conduct.

Religious institutions—the Religions—are necessary. Each represents a way of life that has healed, consoled, and inspired generations of men. But today, the religiously minded must look beyond the institution and the denomination. They must say: Does it express in its creed and in the conduct of its affairs, the ideal it voices? Does it produce the disciplined, sensitive, and useful human being, the only truly religious person? We must be critical of it with the critical spirit of love, with the determination that our temples, churches, and cathedrals shall more adequately testify to the deathless truths of religion and more profoundly influence men to realize those truths in human relations.

We not only have a common enemy; we have a common heritage. The beliefs we share are more important to preserve than those on which we differ.

One of the most dramatic religious achievements of the last quarter century in our country has been that so many Protestants, Roman Catholics, and Jews have come to realize that all of us are seeking a common goal, described in the Judaeo-Christian tradition as the Kingdom of God. A unique pattern has been established in American life, where the winds of free, natural, and democratic intercourse blow over the fences and walls that divide the racial, cultural, economic, political, and religious groups within our diverse population.

I shall never forget the conference in Oxford, England, in the summer of 1946, which laid the foundation for what has now become the World Brotherhood Movement. A hundred representatives from all of Western Europe and the Scandinavian lands were present. Unfortunately, there were no delegates from the peoples "behind the iron curtain." One evening program was devoted to reports from the various countries on the possibilities of inter-faith cooperation. The distinguished international company present was greatly interested in the increasingly effective activities of the British Society of Jews and Christians, in the cooperation of Jews and Christians in Switzerland which alleviated so much misery among the refugees from Nazi Germany; in the first efforts for inter-faith understanding being made in France, Italy, South Africa, the Low Countries and Scandinavia. Everyone who addressed the gathering referred with feeling to the lessons which had been learned in the common suffering during the Nazi occupation. Particularly moving was the contribution of the German pastors, their sense of guilt at what had taken place, their open confession of shame and self-reproach, their determination to start the work of inter-faith cooperation through active effort to dispel ignorance and break down suspicion and prejudice, a work which has since begun in many cities in Germany where branches of World Brotherhood have been organized by Protestant, Roman Catholic, and Jewish leaders, lay and clerical.

Most of all, I shall never forget the open-mouthed wonder of all the delegates as they listened to the contribution of the American delegation. On the platform were rabbi, priest, and Protestant minister, educator and sociologist, as well as other laymen of the three denominations, who discussed differences, irritations, points of friction and misunderstanding among the creeds. It was the familiar panel discussion, characteristic of the technique of the National Conference of Christians and Jews. Delicate themes on which the group felt keenly, subjects which were sore spots, were faced frankly yet without rancor and without compromise of principle by anyone. Behind all the differences and through the entire panel discussion, giving it an earnestness which was compelling, was the theme: We are inheritors of a great tradition, the Judaeo-Christian tradition which accepts the fact of God in the universe, the dignity and freedom of man and the obligations of religious faith to promote human brotherhood.

Again and again these last years Catholic, Protestant and Jew have stood side by side in the struggle for a just economic order. This is something new in the world. The finest men among all groups in our country have come to see that while there are many necessary differences which must be recognized and accepted, the objectives of the three great faiths are the same: the creation of such a society as shall guarantee to every human being the fullest opportunity for self-realization, so long as the welfare of the whole is maintained and advanced.

Everyone of us has had the experience of sorrow. When we walk through the valley of the shadow, when we look at life and men through tears, somehow a new perspective comes into the picture, a sense of time and history. Unimportant things which hitherto assumed such great proportions shrink to their true size, and important things which had been reduced to smallness in the heat of our passions, grow to their true dimensions. The death of a friend or a loved one civilizes us if only for a few brief hours. Our sharp judgments, our cocksure pride of opinion, the clean-cut lines we are so prone to draw between ourselves who are utterly right and those others who are utterly wrong, are shadowed over, melt, and intermingle. How stupid our vanities appear. Where we thought there was no common ground, we see large areas where we can walk and work together with those who differ from us. The spirit is humbled.

Humility is a necessity, not a virtue. Not the arrogant humility of the religious totalitarian who can be just as brutal as the political totalitarian.

There is no true religion without humility. That is taught by Christianity, by Judaism and by the Muslim faith. Moses is described as meek and Jesus as a humble man. Moses in anger broke the first two tablets of the Law, and Jesus in his anger drove the money changers from the temple. In Jewish tradition, Moses offered his life for his people and in Christian theology, Jesus sacrificed his life for the redemption of mankind.

The followers of all the Religions have given verbal assent to these convictions; they have, however, fought among themselves and with each other, not for the universals enjoined upon them, but for the particularistic, losing strength in these controversies, exhausting their idealism in battles for precedence and power and privilege, when they should have been pooling their resources and laboring together to build the city of God. Dare we hope that in our troubled times, men and women in church and synagogue, in mosque and shrine will rededicate our religious institutions to the universal dream?

In the United States Jews and Gentiles are living together, working together, some of them even praying together. Who can predict what will result from this easy, natural intercourse? Perhaps something greater and nobler than our present concepts of Christianity and Judaism, something which will transform both. This need not make for the extinction of either, but for the exaltation of both—each after its own genius.

An especial and solemn responsibility rests upon Gentiles and Christians. They are in the majority. They have the power. Theirs will be the final word which will determine the future. No matter how great an effort at self-purification Jews may make, unless the Gentile majority meets that effort with a parallel manifestation of cleansed hearts and open minds and a rededication to the universal Christian ideals, what Jews may do will be as nothing. Only a genuine acceptance of the spirit of Jesus as the way and the life will bridge the gap between Christian and Jew.

Let us have daring and original thinking, fearless self-criticism. Light must be let into the dark places of the unconscious, where the immediate responses make their home, sometimes breaking into the conscious and controlling it. In the long years that are behind us during which man has fought magnificently against the elemental animal passions of suspicion, prejudice, hate, and mad anger, he has achieved just as magnificently. Now and again the brute from which he came and which he has beaten down again and again, rose to dominate; and in the struggle to beat it down again, much that had been builded and won, was lost. But the caverns are opening, the light creeps gradually into the black corners. Ghostly shapes of old evils slink back and the legions of darkness retreat. This is no messianic dream, no Utopian *ignis fatuus*. It is a sober, realistic appraisal of the pilgrimage of man on earth. The end is not around the corner of another year or another generation. We are speaking of unfolding processes which need long periods of time for their ultimate consummation. There will be stumblings and hesitations, regressions and setbacks. They shall not rob us of our dream.

We are blazers of new trails and hewers-out of new paths for men to walk in. We know that we are struggling against the mistakes, pretenses and prejudices of centuries. But we know, too, that we are making a beginning and others, perhaps stronger than we, shall take our places and carry on, an increasing number in the age-old struggle to put down the brute in man, to elevate what is divine in him, till the last battle is won and the sons of God walk the earth together in justice and in peace.

Our citizens have been divided many times on many issues. Some of these issues are internal; some are rooted abroad. We must learn that loyalties that stretch across the seas must not divide us against each other. Skillful demagogues play upon the feeling of American citizens for this or that or other cause. We shout at each other and call each other names. All sorts of poisons imported from Europe infect us, fever us with suspicions and hates. Is it too much to ask that we be pro-American? No loyalty to a cause beyond the seas is greater than our loyalty to our own country. And that loyalty stands on its own. It cannot, it may not, it must not be identified with loyalty to another group or land or church or people. I do not mean by this that in the United States we should cultivate an exclusive and chauvinistic nationalism. I mean we should strive for a national unity, justified by the threat to freedom, chastened and restrained by a sense of the international responsibility our great power places upon us.

In an article in *The Christian Century*, May 11, 1955, Winburn T. Thomas, commenting on the Bandung Conference declared:

"America's foreign policy must reflect sympathy and understanding. Foreign aid, for all the good it does, is provoked not to help people in need but to combat communism, and thus is immediately mistrusted. A reorientation of national policy requires not a new secretary of state or the location of a few sensitive ambassadors in key capitals . . . Communism succeeds by exploiting hurts, broken hearts and deferred hopes. In opposing communism America thus finds herself at odds with those whom communism claims to be helping. America cannot succeed in her basic hopes for the world until she has demonstrated true fellow feeling for its peoples, their fears and their frustrations. This should have been clear all along. Bandung has writ it large."

America will have a new dynamic, one such as it needs, when we see through the mists of propaganda the issues that are really at stake, when we are prepared to think straight and talk frankly, when we appraise objectively and feel keenly the results of that appraisal. Then we shall know what sort of nation we want to be. And not until then is there any likelihood that we shall have the united national determination to be it.

From the day man began to think critically he has given himself to a consideration of how to change things as they are and fashion them to fit his dream of how they should be. Moses and Jesus kindled fires of aspiration for a just and humane social order which have never been quenched. This age-old quest has lifted human spirits to deathless hope in the possibilities of human existence on this earth. We are in that tradition. Men have died for it;

men are dying for it now. We are the last links in that tradition. It shall not die with us.

We know the sort of world a victory for Communist imperialism would bring. We know it is not the kind of world we want. Our blessed land could never live in peace in such a world. Nor could it develop its true genius.

We want a nation and a world that respect the sanctity of individual and nation and which create instrumentalities to maintain that respect. We want the kind of nation and world that offer to the individual civil and political rights without regard to race, creed, or color; economic security—that is, the removal of the threat of unemployment; an increasing measure of education and leisure and opportunity for its enjoyment; and freedom of conscience and religion. We want that nation and world not for ourselves alone, but for all peoples as well! We want the kind of a world that offers to every nation integrity of its frontiers, its political, economic, and cultural independence, these to be guaranteed by international law, recognized and accepted and implemented by a federation of free peoples. We want this kind of world not for ourselves alone, but for all peoples as well. We want the only kind of nation and world in which peace will endure, a world that accepts justice and compassion as spiritual values that lie at the heart of life, because we believe that "the work of righteousness is peace and the effect of righteousness, quiet and confidence forever." But such a world will not come to us as a gift. We shall have to work for it and sacrifice for it. Thus, while we must concentrate our efforts on the things we are struggling against, we dare not lose our hold upon the things we are struggling for. Men hesitate and falter before the mists which shroud the road ahead. This might be the great moment for church and synagogue to rekindle the lights on the ancient altars; to proclaim once more the Judaeo-Christian ideal—men as their brother's keeper and the work of righteousness is peace.

What ideals are so powerful that when they grip a man they transform him? The reality of God, the dignity of man, man's responsibility to God and his fellowman. When we believe that we are not alone in the world, that somehow all we dream of and hope for is underwritten, that we do not chase illusions, that there is worth in sacrifice, and glory in duty, and magic power in love; when we believe that God is, that we are His children and can deserve His love—a strange new strength comes to us. These are the ideals of the Judaeo-Christian tradition. It is the task of religion to proclaim them, to teach them, to promote them.

These ideals are just as real and practical today as they were when they were first uttered by the Hebrew prophets from Moses to Jesus. On the smaller stage of their day, individuals pursued their own selfish way; there were the classes and the masses, the rich and the poor, the slave and the free. Insincerity, greed, hypocrisy, and corruption degraded their lives. Nations strutted, held themselves to be superior to other nations, and trusted in the power of their arms.

The same abuses plague our world today, but we call them by other names. We fight against the dominance of tyranny in the world, and for the freedom of all peoples. We fight against racial superiority and all the brutalities that flow from it, and for the equality of all men and peoples, of all creeds and colors. We fight against selfish imperialism and all the oppressions it entails, and for the right of nations to express their genius, develop and dispose of their resources and govern themselves so long as they live as good neighbors.

These ideals involve the solution of difficult and complicated problems about which men feel keenly; they involve vested interests and accepted patterns of thought and conduct. They have to do with the treatment of our own Negroes and our fellow citizens who are red or yellow; they have to do with the claims of empire and the rights of weak peoples; they have to do with group prejudice and tension within the nations; they have to do with opportunities for the masses of men to have work at fair wages and a chance for leisure; they have to do with the recognition of individual ability, hard work, acceptance of responsibility and adequate reward therefor; they have to do with the privileges of citizenship and its proud obligations; they have to do with the responsibility of the strong for the weak, of great peoples for small peoples. They have to do with the processes of education, with the training not only of the body and the mind but the disciplines of the spirit which make men choose the decent and honorable.

These universal ideals of the great Judaeo-Christian tradition offer the dynamic by which a more enduring peace may be wrested from the heartbreaking uncertainties of the present.

This is the task of religion: to see to it that peace shall be written in its spirit and underwritten by the will and fervor of believers; to see to it in the name of the living God that no basic human rights shall be ruthlessly destroyed. If men who say they believe in God—His Fatherhood—and in man's brotherhood, lived as if that belief were true, a great revival of the spirit could transform our world. This is what Moses and Jesus were talking about.